MY FIRST WHITE FRIEND

PATRICIA RAYBON

MY FIRST
White FRIEND

Confessions on Race, Love,
and Forgiveness

VIKING

VIKING

Published by the Penguin Group
Penguin Books USA Inc., 375 Hudson Street,
New York, New York 10014, U.S.A.
Penguin Books Ltd, 27 Wrights Lane,
London W8 5TZ, England
Penguin Books Australia Ltd, Ringwood,
Victoria, Australia
Penguin Books Canada Ltd, 10 Alcorn Avenue,
Toronto, Ontario, Canada M4V 3B2
Penguin Books (N.Z.) Ltd, 182–190 Wairau Road,
Auckland 10, New Zealand

Penguin Books Ltd, Registered Offices: Harmondsworth, Middlesex, England

First published in 1996 by Viking Penguin, a division of Penguin Books USA Inc.

10 9 8 7 6 5 4 3 2 1

Grateful acknowledgment is made for permission to reprint an excerpt from "To a White Girl" from *Soul on Ice* by Eldridge Cleaver, McGraw-Hill, 1968. By permission of The McGraw-Hill Companies.

LIBRARY OF CONGRESS CATALOGING-IN-PUBLICATION DATA
Raybon, Patricia.
    My first white friend / Patricia Raybon.
        p.   cm.
    ISBN 0-670-85956-7
    1. Racism—United States.   2. United States—Race relations.
3. Raybon, Patricia.   I. Title.
E185.615.R35   1996
305.8'00973—dc20   95-26232

This book is printed on acid-free paper.

Printed in the United States of America
Set in Granjon

FOR MY FATHER, BILL

I love you more than my own skin.

Frida Kahlo

... And white snow, white mountains, and white faces.

James Baldwin

Take this as a diary. Or a journal. Or a journey:

A long ride back, with stops along the way to sort things out—then forgive them, then forget them. Then it's time to move on.

CONTENTS

MY FIRST
WHITE FRIEND

PROLOGUE

A Confession

It is the moment of truth. I cannot lie to me.
Duke Ellington

God help me.

I stopped hating white people on purpose about a year ago. I didn't tell anybody. I couldn't. If I did, I would have to explain how I started hating in the first place. And I really didn't know then myself.

I just hated.

I hated deeply and smoothly and naturally. I hated in general, and I hated in specifics. I hated with a pure assurance that I had a right to hate—believing that not to hate was itself unpure, and probably unnatural too.

So I hated quietly and politely and pleasantly and I smiled a lot. That is my style—smiling. I was reared to smile, to be polite, to say please and thank you and not to act ugly. I was reared to be the cleanest, nicest, smartest, kindest black child I could possibly be. That would make people like me. White people especially would approve of me. And white people, above all, it was understood, were important and prevailed. So for forty years, and for white people, I was clean and nice and smart. And the effort of it—the sheer idiocy of it—made me utterly and thoroughly sick. Mentally sick, certainly—I was a mess of hypocrisy, facade, and confusion. And physically sick, possibly, too. Indeed, if hate and stress are synonymous—perhaps symbiotic—my body responded accordingly. My medicine chest was full.

But this isn't a medical story.

This is a story about obsession. About compulsion. About annoyance. About an itch that I'd scratched and worried and picked at so long I was bloody in my soul from the worry and rattle of it.

Because the itch made me stupid. It made me a stranger to myself, even hate myself. It made me insecure and paranoid and penitent—trapped by an emotion, a psychological gnawing, that never ever let me rest, that always left me dazed half the time, and weary the other half.

And I thought my soul would die from it. It was killing me anyway—this race-focused consciousness—because it confined my spirit and my vision and my sanity too. And I felt pathological—as confused and mixed up as some white sociologists have always claimed African Americans naturally are.

And naturally, indeed, I thought the problem was with me.

I didn't realize, as James Baldwin observed, "It is very difficult—it is hazardous, psychologically personally hazardous—for a Negro in the country really to hate white people."

Black people are too involved with white people, "not only socially but historically." And indeed, in America, where "we had our slaves on the mainland," as he put it, the uneasy coexistence that some still call a melting pot—but which is more accurately a boiling stew—left me reeling from the pressures of trying to stay cool. And clean. And dry.

While I smiled.

And I knew I had to escape it.

I had to stop hating—because I had to start living.

Before I got old and died and my bones turned white, then turned to dust, I had to live at least one day without seeing white and feeling hate.

And the idea scared me like crazy.

It would be easier to stop breathing. To stop hating *white* people?

It would be easier to cut off my legs. To jump off a cliff. To fly to the moon, flapping my dark arms like some silly bird's bony wings.

Stop hating *white* people?

White people—that relentless, heavy presence. Never benign. Never innocent. "White people" as a category embodied in my view a clear and certain evil—an arrogant malevolence—that had done unspeakable things that I couldn't ignore because I knew the facts of these things. Names and dates and numbers. And the facts haunted me and the numbers justified my hate for all the evil that I believed white people had done.

I knew the stories. I had heard them in childhood, at the knees of people I loved, in the presence of people I trusted. Terrible stories. Horror stories.

White people had murdered Emmett Till and Mack Charles Parker and Medgar Evers and Herbert Lee and the four little girls in the Birmingham church. And white people had acquitted the guilty.

And white people had killed 6 million Semites and enslaved 15 million blacks (and sacrificed 30 million more, some say, to make the passage), and they had broken 400 treaties and irradiated islands and deserts and seas and even people. And they had robbed treasures. And they had reduced by 9 million through death and disease and denial the Iroquois and the Mohawk and the Pequot and the Oneida and the Seneca and the Arapaho and the Navajo and the Cherokee and the Ute and the other Indian populations in North America to a remnant now of barely 1 million. And white people had stolen land and wealth and ideas and music and inventions, and broken promises and backs and treaties and will, and white people had stolen hope.

And I hated white people for all of it.

Hated them because they had lynched and lied and jailed and poisoned and neglected and discarded and excluded and exploited countless cultures and communities with such blatant intent or indifference as to humanly defy belief or understanding.

These are the things I was taught. And these are the things I would learn, in some cases firsthand—as dark children often do.

So for the pain of these things and for the hurt of these things, for declaring black and brown and red and yellow a terrible thing to be, and having the power to enforce that belief—I hated them and I hated their ways, even their means and their deeds.

Their Grandfather Clause and their Virginia Code and their Dred Scott rule and their Group Areas Act and their Plessy Doctrine and their poll taxes and their pass laws and their

Executive Order 9066 and their Edict 44-91 and every other word or deed or intent that they devised to shackle the lives and prayers of defenseless people—I hated them good and I hated them hard.

Quietly I hated, with a silence that too many of us hide behind nice smiles—that expression of oppression. That grin of powerlessness.

A grotesque—that was me.

Grinning and agreeing and smiling and waving, I was the most agreeable hater I know—quiet and mannerly and middle-class and smiling—then, repairing to my neat little home with my neat little manicured lawn and my neat little manicured flower beds, I hated with a mannerly vengeance that wasn't neat, but was wild and messy and ugly because it was trapped inside of me, and was an integral part of me—so much so that I didn't recognize it as hate, but as some kind of justifiable indignation.

"Racial feelings"—that was my description for this state of mind. So that made this consciousness higher than hate. Better than hate. Something noble. Something defensible.

So I could persist with this attitude that, ironically, if ever reversed, could then at any minute swing around and hurt me, and for a curious reason:

Hate for white people had driven me to do nearly everything "positive" I had ever achieved in my life: straight A's back in grade school, so that on Honors Day at the end of the school year the honorees wouldn't all be white and blond; National Honor Society membership, for the same reason; two college degrees; professional honors and awards; publication in national magazines; home ownership in the suburbs, where my perfect house and perfect children and perfect manners allowed me to snub my nose and bare my teeth while I smiled at my unsuspecting suburban neighbors—white people every one.

Racial "duty," indeed, propelled me. But white people controlled me. They were my masters—my neighbors, my bosses, my schoolmates, the store clerks, the doctors, the judges, the coworkers, the others who, in their "whiteness," held over me a mythical, ineffable power. And this power—to define and ascribe and legislate and subjugate—and those who wielded it were everywhere.

I was only chattel.

I lived my life chained to them—bound to their potential to circumscribe everything I did or didn't do, even if I argued that they didn't have that power, or that it didn't matter. But of course it mattered because almost everything I did, or didn't do, was in response to them.

So my dilemma became obvious: If I stopped hating white people, what then would I become? Could I become just myself?

Could I talk loud? Or throw back my head and fall out laughing? Not in front of white people. That was too "colored," and being "colored" was always an unpardonable sin.

So I learned very early that my "self" was unacceptable. And that lesson, expressed in a hundred subtle ways as I moved through childhood and into adulthood, was depraved and unholy. Because it made me a fool and a puppet—acting, reacting, performing, withholding pieces of my identity to protect myself from their reaction or indifference, claiming all the time that I wasn't doing what I was, in fact, doing very deliberately: betraying my "loyalty," as Richard Wright put it, to myself.

So my hair was ironed and my speech was clipped and my manners were bound and chaste and perfect. Thus I was comfortable to them—but a stranger to myself. That "self" was pushed so far down behind my facade she had nearly perished, suffocated under the weight of my duplicity.

And I longed to revive her, to once again give her life, to make her—to make *me*—once again free.

But that meant giving others—white people included—that same freedom, to be something in my mind other than a catalyst or a caricature or a problem. Because white people, taken one-on-one—and not in the abstract, or as a group—were hardly that at all.

They were remarkably ordinary, in fact—just living and crying and hurting and loving like everybody else. They failed and they hoped and they prayed. And they sinned. And so did I.

I needed to trust that to be true, even if I wanted for years not to believe it.

And if that was true—if white people were as unremarkable as me; if they weren't any more or less than I was—then my charge was clear: I could not walk around anymore distracted by what "white people" did or said or sanctioned or tolerated from people who look like me. Because to care meant to lose myself. And to cheat myself. And to betray myself. And that cost was too high.

It cost too much to talk right, look right, smell right, be right, do right, respond right, protest right—"right" meaning being as close as possible to being white. But at the same time, and more important, "right" meaning being as close as possible to being black "in the right way."

Instead I had the nerve to want to just be myself.

Not apart from my ethnicity, but in addition to my ethnicity. I wanted to declare my "self," so I could declare the "selfs" of others.

And maybe, as Baldwin said, "if one could accept the fact that it is no longer important to be white, it would begin to cease to be important to be black."

But that is a dangerous view—a heresy—so I am a renegade.

Because to be somebody in addition to one's ethnicity was a direct challenge to a society that always defines ethnicity as one's entire self, and indeed always in relationship to a white counterweight.

And I can't hoist that monkey around anymore. It weighs too much.

It hides my individuality and denies me the right to see the individuality of others—whites and blacks alike, and brown and yellow and red folks, too. And if I deny the individuality of others, I deny their humanity even as I diminish the humanity of myself.

So I die inside.

Or I choose life.

So I started to write.

A naive and foolish thing.

I started to write—not as I've always written as a newspaper journalist. I started writing about being black in a society where, as Baldwin, again, says, "all you are ever told about being black is that it is a terrible, terrible thing to be."

I had to look at that surreal phenomenon—to get it all down on paper, to look at myself and my past—my family, my faith, my history, my culture, my emotional geography, and also the hate my experience had engendered.

At age forty, indeed, I started the crazy work of peeling back history—my own, my family's, my country's—and writing about it, usually in personal essays.

I sold every one.

So I thought they were good, those little pieces—those sweet, soft memory plays, treading lightly, nicely soothing.

But they were lies.

Not in fact, but in spirit. They positioned me as saintly in racial matters, satisfied and holy. But I was angry and wounded, not ready for healing. So the ruse almost worked. I fooled a few others, and I thought I'd fooled myself.

But truth can't lie down. In a piece about love—of course, it would be love—I slipped. Wrote something real. Showed some true color. Talked about black men and their women, and white men and theirs. Dangerous territory. Talked some more—about black men bedding white women. Then marrying those women. Then leaving black women behind. Dangerous territory. So I excused myself in that piece, blaming as always my "racial feelings." Then I rushed away. Lit the blaze and walked off.

But angry people wouldn't let me.

"You racist bigot!"

"Hey, dark baby! You nigger hypocrite!"

I got mail that could fry ice. Hate mail packs power, like wattage, and I couldn't ignore it. Some mail I pulled from trash bags, saving it as proof it was real. Some I just held in my hands, reading it over and over, not for masochism, but for insight.

These letters were showing me something so simple I could have missed it. Hate doesn't fix anything. It might feel good to hate—and it does sometimes. Sometimes hate is sweet juice, stuff to get drunk on.

But in the morning there's that headache, and that churning mess in the stomach. So a remedy has to go deep. Deep like redemption. Or like hope. Or like forgiveness.

And forgiving people were egging me on. They sent letters, too.

"Please dig deeper into this vein," a middle-aged white Midwesterner wrote, his letter typed carefully on plain white paper, and others sent their own brave urgings.

In my den, I read these letters—some with postmarks from towns I'd never known, from places I'd never seen—but they were all saying the same thing: I am ready to forgive.

And ready to be forgiven.

Ready to open our nation's wound and let it drain and help it heal—to "try again," a woman in Kentucky wrote, not just in racial matters, "but in other areas of my life. I think it's all connected."

This longing was a rudder, steering me relentlessly toward racial reconciliation.

And naturally I resisted that longing with all the strength and will I could summon. Because it asked me to consider the unlikely prospect of saving my life—if not my soul—by rejecting a racial agenda and embracing forgiveness for people I have always identified as "enemy."

Some days I want to turn back. Most days.

Because to practice forgiveness I will first have to forgive myself. Then my family. Then my history. Then I'll have to forgive white people—for being white. And myself for being black. And forgive people who don't think they need forgiving, who'll censure me for daring to believe I have the power to forgive them—and that they need to be absolved.

I'll have to defend myself to people who view forgiveness as a cowardly response to horrific infractions.

But those are small viewpoints.

The larger one is more dangerous. It's the most provocative possibility for a racial scenario: that a person of one race can find a way to love a person of another.

Not eros love necessarily—although that must certainly, indeed, occur. But also agape love—unconditional and divine and raucously forgiving. Undying love. The kind of love that absolutely requires a change of heart. Love that's made by choice, not by chance.

But harder still is self-love. That is the real matter. And it takes a harsh spotlight.

The glare is blinding, requiring me—in my own case—to look at a good family that nevertheless rarely spoke the word "love." That family, at the same time, for all its genuine goodness and support—its high morality, based on sound values—nevertheless never hid its hate. So while our love was always rather murky, our hate—our weariness and our dismay with white people and their institutions—was undeniably clear.

And that kind of clarity is tough to alter. It asks a change of mind and heart that is certainly ludicrous.

It is insanity.

A crazy thing, love.

"We love you madly," Duke Ellington told his fans in Berlin and Biloxi and Buffalo or wherever he played. And the insanity of risking love for people whose acceptance of him was built on the sound of a few sweet musical notes was mad indeed.

But it was vital love. It was air and water.

"I love you more than my own skin," the Mexican artist Frida Kahlo confessed to her lover/husband Diego Rivera, and the shock of her statement was audacious—insanely so—considering that the bulk of her artistic expression, some 200 lushly anguished paintings, her *autoretratos,* is self-portraits. Moreover, Rivera—a notorious philanderer—dishonored his wife's "self" time and time again. But she loved him anyway.

"... more than my own skin."

Love that big transcends self. It must certainly transcend race. It doesn't trivialize race; it rewrites its context. And the effect of that shift, of course, is to liberate the most compelling emotional force—human love.

That is what I seek: love for my human family, and for my immediate family, starting with love for myself. A large and frightening task.

But one piece of it is harder still:

Talking about that love.

Saying it out loud. Risking love—then announcing it, confessing it.

Have *I* told you that I love you?

Indeed for me, confessing my love—for anyone, let alone for people who racially are different—has been the most difficult of expressions because love is wild territory.

It's where people who don't have control go and linger. Love is a place of surrender. Of abandon and trust. And trusting any human being requires from any of us both a love of self and a loss of selfishness. And, ironically, that love of self, at the same time, makes self secondary—or, in my case, makes race *not* primary but, more important, makes race incidental.

Finding the self inside the skin.

Heresy and risk and truth in one package.

A package of juju. Some magic, simply, to get whole and stay sane.

A book on racial forgiveness.

God help me. Because as I weigh the implications of it, and the potential of it, I clearly understand that the philosophy is provocative and good—but I know some people will hate me for it. Some will praise me for it. And some will censure me for it, or even rudely ignore me, deeming me desperate or dumb, or both. But I welcome any response even as I am resigned to it, because I am determined now to understand how my hate started, then figure finally how to slay it. Because hate has hurt me good over these long years. It has crippled me and cheated me and mugged me and left me scarred and impotent and dumb.

And if hate has done those things to me, it has done those things to millions like me.

I see those others every day. They are walking around dead or dying or dumbstruck—on needles and egos, in churches and on dance floors, at corners and in courthouses, at jobs and shops and temples, in tents and palaces, in the air and on the land and on the sea. They are everywhere people are living and breathing and having their being—everywhere people are dazed and hurting and confused. And that is everywhere on this earth.

Victim. That is our name. But we can't wear that label anymore. Don't fit, that label.

Don't fit because it isn't humanity's destiny to be stupid and lost. And if that is true for blacks, it certainly is true for whites still "imprisoned and enthralled," as W. E. B. Du Bois observed, by the "phantasy" of superiority and entitlement.

So I will argue my case against victimhood—for all of us, but first for myself.

I will tell some stories.

Storytelling is the best way I know to make my witness—then to release forgiveness from the confines of theology and dogma and academia, and also from the tyranny of fear—then examine it for myself, then share the journey with ordinary people: all of us, as we are, naked and waiting.

So I will write this book. I must trace my journey from rage to racial reasoning, from hate to love, even from enemies to friends.

I will take a deep breath and open a vein.

A flood can sometimes heal.

God help me.

Let the rains fall down on me.

PART ONE

Race

CHAPTER ONE

A History with Demons

Most things are born in the mothering darkness and most things die.
    Zora Neale Hurston, Moses Man of the Mountain

None of it ever surprised me.

That's the odd thing.

That year when I turned eight, the good things seemed normal. But so did the bad things. So it seemed natural for a white man to be standing on his porch, yelling at children, pointing his rifle at the Colorado sky.

Somebody screamed a warning.

"He got a gun!"

The children took off running—our coattails flapping, our school papers flying from our arms, our galoshes pounding the snow—our skinny legs pumping, racing hard from the worst sight we'd ever seen: a white man with a weapon.

This was 1957 in Denver on Columbine Street, half a block from the elementary school. And those first minutes after school let out, on this day, turned up a miracle: a white man to mess with. He was one of the last white people still in the neighborhood. A natural target. We couldn't help ourselves.

Some older kids had started it, hurling snow at the man's front door and yelling taunts with each crash of a hard snowball. I watched, excited, with kids my age, third- and fourth-graders most of us. I was courageous that day. Surely my parents would've beat me nearly half to death for such foolishness, but I was watching anyway—and laughing and whooping every time a snowball crashed—bam!—into the man's front door.

Then the door flew open and an old man was on his porch, angry and yelling and God almighty pointing a *gun*.

Everybody took off running. Screaming but laughing too, and falling down and scrambling up and falling again and laughing even more. We were kicking up snow, turning our flight into a footrace, loving the terror because it felt fun. So when we got to the end of the long street and turned the corner safely, we were flushed hot and we were happy. Eight years old and silly and laughing hard, letting the older kids go their way—but glad we'd been there too.

So we fell down, contented, all over each other. Breathing hard and sighing. We dropped our books in the snow, then fell on our backs in the snow, some of us, and watched our breath climb in frosty shapes toward the cold, white Colorado sky. And everything felt so good. The breath going in, and the laughter going out. And the white man angry. It was perfect.

Then one boy jumped to his feet and shouted:

"Let's do it again!"

A crazy idea. Stupid idea. But it pumped up our laughter,

and we rolled around in the snow, hollering again and laughing and squealing. We jumped up ready again to run.

Then one girl grabbed the brave boy by the shoulders, shaking him loose, but laughing with the rest of us.

"You stupid square-head boy. Don't you see nothing? That white man—he got a gun?!"

"I know it!" the boy screamed, laughing, his voice cracking. "I know it!" And he fell to his knees in the snow, holding his stomach because he had a stitch in his side.

Then he rolled to his feet. He grabbed a stick and started mimicking the man with the gun:

"You damn kids! Get off my yard! Get off my fence! I said GET OFF MY FENCE! GET OFF MY YARD!

The boy's breath escaped in white bursts. He snorted out laughter and steam, and the other children picked up the chant, blowing out words and frost and screaming laughter at each other, churning our breath skyward.

GET OFF MY FENCE! GET OFF MY YARD!

We made a parade. We marched to our houses, pounding our galoshes on the ice, kicking up slush, shouting with glee.

GET OFF MY FENCE! GET OFF MY YARD!

Our screams echoed off the cold snow and we were a band of frigid breath and happiness. We waved to each other and shouted joyfully good-bye.

Then at home, a lovely feeling warmed us.

What a good day.

What a perfect day.

A white man felt some pain.

That was a good thing? Even at age eight, we knew it.

Even in Colorado, with all that big sky—all that blinding

white sun, all that soft air and lovely trees and lovely summers—even with all of that, we knew that pain for any white man was a wonderful thing. Even in Colorado, where, in 1957, a black man could live with his family and almost forget.

So my father, like thousands of others, came after the war, at the turn of the decade in 1951, to behold the illusion. And my father stayed.

He bought his first house, brick with an upstairs apartment he rented out for extra income. And Negroes lived the good life. We had basements and picture windows and porch lights and two-toned doorbells.

We ate picnics on tablecloths. We played Ping-Pong in our basements and badminton on our "lawns."

The worst evil was behind us. We laughed at the devil. We had escaped the South and its madness and its lies. So we were free, and nothing could spoil that, or even put out the sun.

But something went wrong.

Somebody rang up the demon. And we beheld him and we hated him. Despised his very face.

Look for small things. That's what children remember.

I remember the mountains—the white people there—and the trips we'd take on summer holidays and hot Sunday summer afternoons.

We'd leave after church, gliding out from Denver in our Buick, Packard, Nash, Chrysler, Dodge sedans—spiraling past the pine and the aspen and the sunflowers. A caravan of friends and laughing.

The drivers were the men.

Our mother's husbands. Our dearest fathers.

They were thirtysomething and cocky. They had pretty

wives and laughing children. They had a war behind them and fixed mortgages.

And jobs. And college degrees earned at Negro schools back in Georgia and Texas and Missouri and Virginia. And now they were out West in Colorado, living large, with ambition and faith and style.

My father smoked Philip Morris cigarettes in a tortoiseshell holder. He drove his '54 Dodge with one hand on the steering wheel, the other propped on the edge of the open car window. He ordered white men to pump his gas and wash his windshield.

He bought a cowboy hat, wore it low on his brow to shield back the Colorado glare. He was handsome, I thought, in a lean, sinewy way. I loved the smell of him—tobacco and hair pomade and chewing gum. And I revered his attitude: He ruled our world without apology. He never blinked.

I thought he was God.

Once, at the big train station downtown, a white porter nearly ran over my sister with a cart full of luggage. The man didn't look back, didn't apologize. In a second, my father had the man against the cart. He was in the man's face, trembling, every black inch of him, blessing the man out. The man finally found his wits. "I'm sorry! I'm *sorry!*" he said. My father released him, looking disgusted. Then Daddy wiped his hands along his pants legs, wiping away sweat, wiping away the moment.

He had made his point.

That's not the kind of story I'm supposed to tell about my father. When I do, people complain to my mother: Why doesn't Patricia describe his good deeds and his achievements?—which, in fact, were many and impressive. He was a pillar, some days a saint.

But I'm looking for the whole man. And in that entity, I suspect I will find myself and him too—and also answers to the kinds of questions that dark children often ask. The whys and hows. And the why nots. Therefore, whatever he achieved matters more to me in contrast to his whole story, not just its prettiest parts.

With an ache in my heart, indeed, and with great fondness I look back and see him during those early years in Denver. I thought he was beautiful.

Weekdays, he wore blinding white shirts to his government job at the Air Force Accounting and Finance Center. He was an auditor—one of two black men there—a number cruncher with a short haircut, working figures all day on a hand-cranked, government-issue adding machine.

On Saturdays he turned the sleeves back on a clean white shirt and considered it casual. But he was not casual.

This was 1957 and we were Negroes and this was Colorado. And to survive that, or defy it, he put on an armor that made him stern and unrelenting—polite but uncompromising—serious and unforgivingly black. I can see him, years later, in an upscale restaurant, his eyeglasses on his forehead, studying the fancy man's menu with an air of familiarity and entitlement. Then after eating the sumptuous meal—the veal medallions or the cracked lobster, or whatever it was—slightly pushing back his chair and crisply, with a slight smile, telling the waiter: "No dessert for me, thank you. I have dined sufficiently."

I have dined sufficiently.

He spoke English beautifully, "perfectly," with a crisp snap. Whatever black boy's drawl he might have spoken years before in Mississippi and Memphis and St. Louis was long gone. And we—my sister and I—spoke that foreign tongue, like him, almost like natives.

And we held our bodies stiffly to walk like Negroes. We didn't bob or sway or drag. We talked like he taught us and we kept ourselves quiet and clean and orderly because, like him, we had to survive the journey from the old colored life to the new Negro one. And this was important business.

James Baldwin put it this way:

"I realized ... that I really had buried myself beneath a whole fantastic image of myself which wasn't mine, but white people's image of me. I realized that I had not always talked— obviously I hadn't always talked—the way I had forced myself to learn how to talk. I had to find out what I had been like in the beginning."

In the beginning.

My father, Bill, was born poor and early in Walls, Mississippi, a forgettable, dirt-poor enclave just south of the Tennessee border. His mother, Annie Smith, was pretty and fourteen and scared. His Daddy remains a mystery, his name never whispered. Not then. Not now.

So Annie was in charge of her boy.

She gave him her last name. Then she changed my father's birthplace to Memphis, Tennessee, an attempt perhaps to "city-fy" her country baby. That would matter to her. She kicked the country dust off her feet as soon as she was old enough to leave.

Mississippi made her leave. It was a silent, dark forest and empty. And Walls was the end of the world. Nothing but hot days and stray dogs and red dirt. She hated it.

So she fled north with an older sister and never looked back. "If she ever came back to Mississippi, I don't remember it," says Dewitt White, my father's only first cousin.

Dewitt himself left at age seventeen for California and at

seventy-five still lives there—with palm trees and fruit trees and a trove of California memories: like the years he worked in Beverly Hills for a florist whose clients were movie stars. "Judy Garland. Edward G. Robinson. Laraine Day. Loretta Young. One time we worked in Lana Turner's home for ten days doing different decorations and her girl—the one who killed Stompanato—she was a little girl at that time."

These are the details of a family that scattered—because maybe that's what dreamers do when they're desperate.

"It was independence—like a streak of independence," Dewitt says. "The whole family has it. Everybody kind of followed their own dreams, just picked up and took off."

Or they were driven, by their one deep and abiding belief: They were better than poor Mississippi white folks.

"Crackers" they called them—with a disdain that those whites felt equally only for "niggers." Poor folks hating poor folks.

No hate runs deeper.

One branch of the family still brags today "that none of them ever worked for nobody white." Dewitt says this. It's a badge of honor. They all started their own businesses—trucking, hauling, carpentry, construction—anything to keep from working for a poor white boss man.

My grandmother Annie was cut from this fabric. She was scared—not because she had a baby—but because she knew motherhood could trap her in Mississippi poverty, leave her no better off than a cracker.

Escape meant leaving Mississippi, and the outhouses and the cotton fields and the red dust. Fleeing north to the city—working sixteen to eighteen hours every day—pressing and curling black folks' hair, scrubbing and waxing white folks' houses. Smiling at white folks and forbearing them just the same. But this was OK. She was creating something.

She was rising. And she wouldn't stop, not until long years later when, finally, at forty-seven she, too, bought her own business—a corner variety store in north St. Louis.

Bought it with her own money, $305 "plus inventory," in 1948. Bought the store from a white woman. Bought it because the white woman was raped in that store. A black man raped her, and she sold the store to Annie for a song. And Annie didn't flinch. She paid the money and changed the name and stood behind the counter with her pencil and her sharp eye and her quick laugh selling her penny candy and canned sardines and sausages and cold sodas at a markup, and she knew she'd finally made sweet and made good. And she never doubted for a day that she'd earned it.

A pretty woman believes, indeed, in inalienable rights. It comes from the approval she gets so effortlessly—for being shapely with smooth brown skin and a dimple. It emerges rather naturally after years of laughing easily and coaxing other people to laugh with her. "She was always so much fun," her nephew, Dewitt, remembers. Without trying, yes, his Aunt Annie convinces people they are blessed to be in her presence. Fearlessly, she announces out loud her dreams because she believes she *should* dream. And why shouldn't she? The cosmos understands ambition. So she isn't embarrassed to tell her best girlfriends that, of course, she will own a business herself one day.

And her boy, once he was grown, was indeed proud of her accomplishment. He'd casually mention, to anybody who'd listen, that he had to do the books for his mother's store in St. Louis. She had a thriving store, he'd say, a variety store bought with her own money from a white lady. Her store now. Such a woman. Yes, she is quite pretty, isn't she?

So young-acting. My mother.

But my Daddy never told me she left him.

I had to find it out long after he was dead and buried. I had to call up old relatives and dig out old papers to find out our truth—the truth of our beginning, the truth of our fates, the truth of our antipathy. And here is the truth: Much of it started in a young girl's heart.

Pretty Annie Smith.

Little brown girl with memories in her bones and a dimple in her brown left cheek. Too many memories for one brown girl to bear. Too much Mississippi history. Too many Mississippi ghosts.

Her little brother's spirit was one of them. It wouldn't settle down and rest.

Because he died so poorly. And Annie was partly at fault. She and her little sister, Eula, had put that rope on him and were just playing around. But he tried to run. Then he fell. And the rope yanked hard on his neck. And the rope burns tore into his yielding young skin and blood poisoning set in and the sepsis was relentless.

He died. A sweet little boy. Just a baby, really. And Eula never could forget. Grieved for him until the day she died. But Annie buried that memory so deep she'd look surprised if somebody mentioned it. She'd cock her head and purse her lips, annoyed that somebody dared to bring up that "accident" from so long ago.

Because now was better. Now was St. Louis—a big town packed with black ambition and dreams—and she couldn't look back. She was young and the town was rich and there were schools for colored hairdressers. And after a time she was working, pressing hair, and making a little money and old enough to marry a black laborer named Henderson. Proudly wearing the title "Mrs." Proudly going to church. Proudly riding the streetcar out to Clayton, sitting in the front seat and daring anybody to make something of it.

Then she'd walk to the white woman's house, wearing pretty street clothes. Not until later would she put on the uniform and pull up her hair and take off her smile. So on the street she looked young and pretty and prosperous—as if she herself could be living like a white lady in Clayton.

But St. Louis wouldn't allow that.

It held her back on the north side of town. Made her hide her face from the pretty shops in Clayton, took her to the back door to pick up deliveries, made her wait outside in the sun while the city smiled and cooed at the white lady in Clayton.

So maybe she hated that lady in Clayton. Hated her with every step, with every breath. Hated her for smoking Luckies and playing canasta while she cleaned the woman's filth and tended the woman's children and cooked the food and baked the cakes for the woman's joyless husband. And every hot, sweaty minute in that white woman's house she dreamed of being something more.

Some days maybe she would dream of her boy and what he'd be when she brought him up north—not a laborer like Henderson, whom she later would divorce. Not a yardman or a chauffeur. Not a janitor with dust in his pretty black hair. Her son would be something important and something great, and she would be too.

So she'd yank off her apron and put on a clean, starched dress and wait in the dusk for her bus and dream her dreams.

She was a queen even then. Talked like one. Dressed like

one. Wore fox fur in her middle age, and later mink, like she was born to it.

Wore Sunday hats like they were crowns.

Fixed her apartment pretty, like in the magazines, with wallpaper and department store slipcovers.

And she dared St. Louis to stop her. She was good as white folks, if not better. And as soon as she could make her meager ends meet, she'd send for her boy. But he'd be safe now in Mississippi with her mother while she worked it all out.

Surely he would be safe. Even if the years went by.

Surely nothing could harm him while he waited.

That's how she saw it.

That's what she chose to believe.

She was wrong.

Mississippi has black earth like the river and red earth like the blood. Too much dying has happened there. Indians and black folks and poor whites slaughtered in war and folly.

My father, in the 1920s, tried to grow up whole in Mississippi, but his mother had left him. And his only grandmother Eliza Jones, for all her Christian intensity, for all her genuine devotion to God and family, "told only one person in the world that she loved him," says Cousin Dewitt, "and that was the Lord."

She loved Jesus. But if she loved anybody else she never told it. Cousin Dewitt is clear on that. "I never heard her say I love you to nobody."

She didn't have time. She never learned. This was Mississippi, a bloody domain of the South. Children could die here. You just trained them and whipped them and prayed.

There is an austere harshness to that kind of atmosphere, and black people know it well. We can blame lynching and white citizens councils and KKK night riders for killing us by the thousands, but nobody knows how many more of us have died in our hearts instead from homes without unconditional warmth and love.

Try loving somebody when nobody else does. It is almost impossible. Try granting acceptance when an entire nation is conspiring against the idea of that. There's no time for such foolishness. There's only time for working through your destiny, however it's shaped. So Eliza Jones worked, and she tried some hours to find leisure, but she couldn't. She was busy overcoming her birth. America requires that of outsiders.

But in time, she made herself a person to reckon with, and she looked the part. She stood six feet tall—a showpiece of African and Negro and Choctaw Indian blood. It was a sin, she thought, to still be in bed when the sun came up. She worked hard as a man, and was as big as most of them.

It makes sense that she caught the eye of George Jones, a "big" Negro over in Abbeville, Mississippi. He owned acres of Mississippi pine and the sawmill that produced his lumber and also carried his name. "He was one of the biggest, most powerful black men in that part of the country at that time." In fact, it was a small corner of the world. But it seemed big to a boy, even to a man now looking back. So Dewitt White, talking about this "powerful" figure, will call up his picture of Jones—a memory that, first, invokes the fact of his skin color. "A light-skinned black man," says Dewitt, "with good-looking stock—lots of 'pretty' children. His father was probably white. George Jones was his name and he owned the trees and the mill and he ran it deep in the country like a slave camp."

Black men worked that mill. And a little black boy.

My father worked that mill.

"Like he was a slave," his cousin says.

From the time he was big enough to haul a bucket, my father worked that mill like a man and endured George Jones and he tried to pull on the love of his grandmother Eliza. But there was little to spare.

And her new husband, George Jones, it turned out, was a tyrant. A brute. Beat the woman and beat the child, too. A little boy living on his place was just trouble anyway. Hardly worth his keep. Just get him up before daybreak and keep him working and make sure he kept his tongue still.

So my Daddy worked and held quiet. And he waited—believing maybe if he worked hard enough his Aunt Eula would come put a tag on him and ship him north to his pretty mother.

Maybe when he was five or six. Or maybe seven. Well, maybe when he was eight, his pretty lady in the photograph would send for him and he would be saved.

Or maybe when he was nine or ten or twelve.

Maybe when he was thirteen, the smiling lady would send the money and ship him north to home. Maybe then he'd get the summons he'd waited for all his life.

And so it came.

Let's call it a good day when he got the news. A great day. But he was scared to death.

I can see the fear. A photo of him taken less than a year after his arrival in St. Louis sits on my desk.

My father at fourteen.

He stands at attention, his face frozen into submission. His body, razor-straight, is encased in a pale wool suit—a jacket with three glass buttons and dress-up city knickers.

A suit from Annie: made to match Annie's vision for her stranger boy. A man's pale suit with a stiff white shirt and a striped tie knotted like jute around his neck. His face is gleaming with oil, his hair brushed hard and flat—every black strand tamed flat on his angular skull.

A clean black child. Never had spare dirt on him anywhere. He couldn't stand dirt. He'd learned that in Mississippi, hated all that damp, red dust. Eliza scrubbed him nearly raw on bath nights, and Annie had the same standard.

She would've groomed him that year, 1926, to match her own image—an image she had pieced and stitched together out of dreams and wonder and a blithe confidence that if she wasn't born great she should have been.

She could forget that just months before her boy was hauling George Jones's lumber in Mississippi, because hard work was a given. And she could forget he didn't know her. That she was a pretty stranger. That he might call her Mother and promise to work hard and love her and go far, but he didn't know what any of it meant.

Smile, she would say, showing her dimple.

But he couldn't.

All the years in Mississippi left my father with a hole in his heart and light-heartedness would never be his lot. Life just wasn't funny to Bill.

He was best only when he was working, because that's what people most expected of him. When he worked, he was a good boy.

Annie expected that. She wanted him polished up and educated and dusted off. His speech straight and his manners right. She wanted him prepared. His life would not be menial and stupid and small. He would not work for white men who called him boy. He would not shuffle and grin when nothing was funny, scratch when nothing was itching. He would work harder than even white men expected him to. And it would pay off in the end.

He would be great.

He would be a Negro.

A Mississippi boy gives up a lot for that. There's his pride, which he swallows because in St. Louis he's put back one year in school. There's his speech, which he adjusts to fit in quickly with the city boys. And soon his speech is more refined than theirs. And he fits in with the other boys, all twenty or so of them who live on his block and make up a tight circle—"the Aldine Gang," named for the street where they lived. He lets them tease him with a nickname, Old Black Bill. He wants to be like them so much. They all have mothers who love them, even spoil them, and fathers with nice jobs.

So he accepts his stepfather, but Mr. Henderson only tolerates him. And he accepts his mother's nickname for him, Jack. But it's never really said with much fondness. It's used mostly when she's angry or irritable. "Jack!" Calling him like a mule. But he comes. He holds his tongue. He does his jobs—cutting white folks' lawns and busing tables at white hotels. He studies hard. He says thank you.

He had waited for this time.

He must endure it. He knows about endurance.

So it goes like this. Working and pleasing Miss Annie.

And over time, she does indeed remake him, like she remade herself—by sheer will. She sent him to high school, then to a Negro college, Lincoln University in Jefferson City, Missouri, where he earned the family's first college degree—a reward for the persistence and hard work that was his trait.

When the General Accounting Office later hired him to

audit government books, and promoted him—but promoted white men quicker—he just worked harder. He even trained white men, who then passed over him for jobs: white boys out of college going to Bill Smith to get trained, then getting promoted and leaving him behind.

So he worked harder. And dressed better. Wore shirts white as ice, stayed more hours then he was paid. Surely that's what they wanted. He was one of the smartest, hardest working auditors at the GAO—that's what they all said, anyway.

One of the best Negroes they had ever seen.

Annie's boy. Jack.

Old Black Bill.

But something was wrong. He couldn't laugh easily.

This business of being a Negro—trying to prove yourself better than white folks, never getting a minute's break from their disapproval—took so much time. So much effort.

And there was no escape. Not even in the Colorado mountains. Up there, at 8,000 or 9,000 or 10,000 feet—white people were still white and he was still black.

At a company picnic, he listened to their jokes, but his smile was pasted on. I watched him play in a men's baseball game, thinking oddly how black my Daddy looked next to all those white men. Certainly they noticed. As hard as he worked, he was still black—which he would say didn't bother him, but he surely knew it worried the white folks because white folks thought black was the worst possible thing to be.

No wonder he never relaxed. Not even with other Negroes did he look at ease to me. On those trips to the mountains, he would join the men and listen to their stories. Colored stories. Nigger stories. Shufflin' stories. Mean tales, many of them, or that's how they sounded to me. Stories that should have made grown men wail and moan up in the Colorado clouds, but instead they laughed and laughed. So hard they cried.

And my father held forth with jokes, too. But back in the car, his face shut down and the smile fell off his lips like the mask that it was.

So why was he laughing minutes before?

Because the lies hurt too much to cry.

The lies were so false that all he could do was laugh. So my father slapped the backs of friends and the men pulled on their smokes and opened up their throats and hollered.

Then they wiped their eyes and lit the charcoal and the mothers tossed the salads and sliced the cakes for later.

And they ignored what had happened minutes earlier.

Earlier we had pulled off the road in our caravan of cars—and we surveyed the picnic grounds. The car doors opened. We emerged.

Car after car of black men from the city—unloading children and wives and blankets and food.

Black men with strong arms and deep voices and big laughs. Our dearest fathers.

And the white men at the camp sites would look up from their chicken and their beer. They'd swallow hard, then call their children and motion to their wives.

And before our fathers could get their gear and their families arranged on the grounds, the white men had loaded up their automobiles and their families and their picnics and they had driven their scared families away.

Not just sometimes.

Every time.

Every sunny Colorado mountain trip ended with our families waving away the dust of white people hurrying away from our presence.

Running like scared deer from dangerous predators.

Unwilling to sit on the same rock and breathe the same air and view the same tree with a man and his family and his friends who happened to be black.

So we watched them go.

We breathed the thin air and we watched them take their leave of us.

This was a small thing, perhaps. But to a child, it was enough of an offense to kindle and nurture a solid hate. People who shun you don't deserve more. That's what I believed then.

But if that wasn't enough to teach me about white people— and it was—we got verbal lessons all the time.

"White people will stop your progress if you let them," my father told my sister and me, "so don't let them."

It felt like an order.

"If they say you can't, you show them you can. They expect the least from you because they don't know who you are. They are ignorant. They will call you gal. They will charge you more money for shoddy goods. They will pay you less than you're worth. And pay themselves more. They will look you in the eye and lie."

Lessons all the time. They came with this life and this color, and Bill made sure we got fresh lessons, it seemed, almost every day.

They weren't deliberate. They just came with living. Every day, white folks did something hateful. So the lessons took. Over time, I couldn't hate white people enough.

We flicked their crumbs from the picnic tables in the mountains and swept their ashes from the grills—wiping away their presence.

Then we spread the tables with the white tablecloths ironed by our mothers—yards and yards, it seemed, of spotless white cotton—and our fathers unwrapped huge blocks of ice and chilled the sodas and beer and crowded fat watermelons into the icy water and tended the meat as it sputtered and popped on the grill.

And the Colorado sun beat down on our heads and it blessed us and we ate.

We ate with a deep hunger and with pain but we laughed through it all. Negroes laughed more than anybody I ever saw.

So did their children.

We hollered and sang, playing hide-and-seek among the tables and the pine trees that the scared white people had fled. Our hair ribbons came undone and, surely, we were wildly happy.

Only years later would we stop laughing long enough to ask our questions and heal our wounds. Wounds as old as Mississippi, filled with sawdust and old ghosts and the dreams and fears of old, black queens. And filled with white people. Big white demons, all named Bogeyman.

We wanted to call up those demons and slay them. I wanted to push them far away and not be afraid of my shadow—a shadow that white strangers especially seemed to hate.

But I didn't have a weapon. I hadn't learned of love— enough to speak of it—so I learned instead to hate them. Learned it good and well. And white people, conveniently, played their timeless role. Fleeing and wailing and screaming and calling us ugly, spiteful names. Just like Annie said they would. And like Bill promised. They were so easy to hate. But surviving them had taken so much time. All of our lives.

Annie, on the last full week of her life, finally considered what the effort had cost her. She'd given the days and the nights of her youth and her middle age—damn near all of them, anyway—to "improving" herself, then proving herself, but she'd done it mostly for pale strangers who, in the end, didn't much care about her achievements anyway. She'd sacrificed the contact and companionship of her only child during his youngest, most tender and formative years—but found out too late that lost years can't often be regained. And love? It takes *time*.

In a letter to my father in Denver, written the Monday before she died—Thanksgiving Day, 1956—after she closed her store for the night, she wrote these words from St. Louis:

"I always feel blue around Thanksgiving and Christmas, because I'm so far from any of my family but I get by somehow and always have . . ."

Get on by, girl.

That's what she did, then it all went up in smoke.

On the night of her funeral—a late evening service on a black November night—her St. Louis apartment building went up in flames.

It was burning when we returned from the funeral. Orange flames lit the night and black smoke choked the air and shrouded her building. Looters had started the job the night she died, emptying the cash register in her store and carrying off her treasures from her apartment. My father had to round up the stuff when he got to St. Louis the next night, knocking on doors and demanding back his mother's little items.

So the mourning had to stop. Just one tear. That's what fell.

It slid down Daddy's cheek—the only one I ever saw him shed—then quickly it was gone.

He had nothing else he could give her then. Not even a gravestone. She's buried somewhere in St. Louis in an unmarked grave. Just a number, that none of us knows, testifies that she was here, and now is gone.

He could've fully forgiven her, and saved us all—forgiven her for leaving his childhood, for not knowing that "racial achievement" is never more important than life itself, for not fully seeing that roots, when severed, leave a spirit unhitched. Forgiven her, indeed, for only doing what black folks have to do: Prove their worth, then survive.

But that takes sacrifices, and he was one of them.

He'd be bemused, indeed, that his own grave is on a grassy knoll in lovely Colorado with only black folks buried there. The cemetery fixed it that way, I guess. On Memorial Days and holidays, the white folks go one way—and we go ours.

Not even death spared him its indignities.

And he worked so *hard*.

Hundreds mourned him on his final day. The obituary was long with accolades and speeches. Pretty words on a cold, sunny morning.

He got that in the end.

Instead, we should have loved him—held him close and told him he was ours. Not with speeches. Or plaques and citations. But with soft hands. With our hearts. But that is hard for hurting people to do, especially when they're busy—making a way out of no way.

He tried to warn me as a child. He held my hand and took me to the mountains. Then he formed the words, in a hundred different ways, that made me understand one hard, important thing:

It doesn't matter that nobody sees your face or knows your name, my wide-eyed child, my father said to me.

You know it. You be it.

You are.

He said these things but he waved away the dust of fleeing cars carrying the fearful and the pale. His gesture spoke volumes, and I read it like a book, understanding exactly what it said: Don't trust them. Beware of them. It's OK to indulge in that deep feeling that sits in the pit of your stomach on most American days, that awareness that somebody's hurting you constantly, so you must respond.

It's OK even to give a name to that sinking feeling. You might even call it hate.

Gestures are that clear and that loud—a body language for people hated for their bodies. A clear signal.

So what else was there to do?

I watched and I listened.

I believed.

I obeyed.

CHAPTER TWO

The Problem Is Me?

The man who sweats under his mask,
whose role makes him itch with discomfort,
who hates the division in himself, is already
beginning to be free.
*Thomas Merton, from "Why Alienation
Is for Everybody," 1969 essay*

If you look hard, you can see fear rising off old soldiers like smoke. But on this day the sun is too bright. The water is glistening.

I cannot see.

We're at "the pool," the new swimming center in northeast Denver, when out of the blue a girlfriend sits up stiffly and frowns at me.

"You're kind of *dark,* Patricia," she says.

Four other little Negro girls, also my friends, are looking now at me, too—nodding in agreement.

We are lying on towels in swim suits, drying in the sun like white people do on TV. I have on last summer's suit that still kind of fits so I hope it makes me look pretty. Then a boy would notice me and say something to tease me. Then I'd laugh and tease him back and that would make me feel pretty and special on this very hot day.

Looking pretty—it is everything I want.

It gets me attention from people, from boys in particular, and I crave that attention—even at the age of nine. Getting watched and admired, getting approval for the way I *look*—and from a male. Nothing makes me feel more affirmed and excited than the positive affirmation of a boy.

That is a fool's confession.

But truth is a balm. And the truth is that, in 1958, my sense of self is dependent totally on how others see me—my physical self.

And boys judge that. Boys decide in 1958 who is pretty. Getting approval from any one of them provides a measure of assurance, and I crave it. But there is irony, of course. My *physical* identity is never neutral. I can never relax in my skin. Colorado doesn't allow that. Negroes are still oddities here.

At nine years old, I am a curiosity in Colorado. White mothers, smiling awkwardly, shield their babies from my touch or stare at me, unsmiling, like they're seeing something dead or rotten.

At nine years old, indeed, I don't know what it is to breathe easy.

Not even on summer afternoons—at the height of the day's play—can I throw on indifference and relax. Instead I'm called into my house by my mother to get cleaned up for my father's return from work.

Every day, just at that hour when the mud and the bicycles and the lawn sprinklers and the best friends might grant me a moment of carefree abandon, my named is called.

"Patricia!"

I then must stop.

I must leave friends and sun.

I must go into the house. I bathe and powder and oil my body and put on a clean playsuit—but I can't play in it—then brush and comb my hair and put on a clean hair ribbon.

Then with my sister, who is also now cleaned up, I can wait on the porch swing next to the geraniums and the marigolds for my beautiful father's return.

He will like to see us this way—cleaned and combed at four o'clock on a summer afternoon when we should be dusty and grimy and smelling like our sweat.

But he is his mother's son. Like her, he can't stand a dirty, smelly child.

Nobody can stand me like I am.

I have to look pretty.

I hope my swim suit still fits and looks good.

I need somebody to tell me I look nice. But the gods, sometimes kind, are today harshly cruel.

"You're really kind of *dark,* Patricia."

I laugh a little, not knowing how else to respond.

My friend, the daughter of one of Denver's elite Negro families, is at nine already old enough to confidently raise this subject—this matter—that we've all learned is important.

Light skin is good.

Dark skin is bad.

In my swim suit, I am exposed as "more" dark than she apparently realized, although "dark" is so relative it's nearly meaningless. Too dark? Dark enough? I can't decipher the fine distinctions.

But I'm desperate for it not to matter.

I turn my back to her and look at the water, pretending interest there. But my eyes can't find a decoy, something to deflect her scrutiny.

The pool is churning with children. The sky is ice blue and so is the water—a sparkling diamond cut by the sun. A lovely pool in our heavenly city.

We should all feel blessed.

But lying side by side on towels with girls I have known most of my life, I am itchy with an awareness that seems stupidly vital: They are all much lighter than me. None is darker than the lightest shade of sweet caramel.

They are the picture of middle-class black Denver in the fifties. It is a world of big cars and big lawns and light-yellow children who swim on hot days in a lovely pool built at their fathers' insistence for our side of town. They are people who have everything and get everything done. They are beautiful and light and their hair doesn't crinkle after it dries at the pool.

I envy them all. I don't know any better.

"Let me see your arm," one of the girls says, and she scoots closer to my towel. She will play a game, and I am the game piece.

"Who's the darkest?" she asks loudly, and presses closer to compare arms. Next to her milky forearms, my brown limbs are dark and hairy. So I try to pull them back close to my body, but five girls hold down my arms—laughing as I struggle—while they show each other how much lighter their skin is compared to mine.

So it's a moot exercise to line up, as one of them suggests, by color—and arrange ourselves on our towels in descending order:

First will be lightest. Last will be darkest.

We jockey for position. They are giggling. I have started to sweat. Then for a few minutes, a debate erupts as the two lightest girls in the group argue about who is the lightest of all.

"No, look," one girl is saying. "The little hairs on my arm make me *look* darker than you are. But I'm really lighter. See?"

She shifts slightly to expose her forearms—hairless and creamy and indisputably whiter than any others in our group.

And that status makes her shine. She is glowing and smiling and serene. Her eyes are closed and she lies back on her towel and reaches up with one hand and releases her pony tail from its clasp and spreads a torrent of silky, dark hair onto her fluffy towel.

She is the queen.

She is pretty.

I am brown—with woolly hair drying like fuzz in the dry Denver heat.

I am the darkest on the towel—and I don't know how to transform myself, or understand that I don't have to.

I pat down my hair with my hands, but the fuzz is stubborn. It springs up in stiff bales all over my head. So I pull on my swim cap and wrap my towel around my body and laugh with them while they laugh at me for my one unforgivable sin: I am the darkest on the towel.

Then they decide all at once to jump back in the water.

Some boys are calling them from the pool. The boys are splashing them and calling their names and teasing them, and the buttermilk girls are all laughing and tossing aside their fluffy swim towels and jumping with their silky hair back into the sparkling, blue water.

Some even jump from the high board—they are all such keen swimmers. So they leap into the air. They soar.

The sparkling water envelopes them in a baptism.

They are blessed.

They are pretty.

They can never drown.

"Did you have fun?"

My mother, in the summer of 1958, can wear shorts and a

halter top and tennis shoes and look natural and logical—and good, too. She has nice legs and an easy laugh and a no-nonsense style. During the school year, she teaches physical education at an elementary school in a modest, northeast Denver neighborhood. She loves the kids and their parents, and is good at making people happy. She likes games and sports and laughter. Having her for a mother is like living with a full-time recreation director. Indeed, my mother's first name—Nannie, which she never has liked—does, in fact, capture her character. She is like a nanny. She embodies caring. She is my mother hen, always nurturing.

She involves my sister and me in every possible organized "opportunity"—Girl Scouts, church choirs, youth clubs, piano lessons, summer camps, swimming programs, ice skating, fashion shows, and outings with the children of Denver's black elite.

But she isn't status conscious as much as she wants us exposed to "the best." Spending an afternoon at a sparkling pool with the children of Denver's black bourgeoisie seems to qualify.

She is pleased when she opens the car door.

Did you have fun?

I love my mother. I don't know how to say that in 1958—I never hear that phrase spoken casually in my house, so I don't know how to tell her in words.

But in 1958, climbing into our '54 Dodge, I love that she cares for my well-being so much that her first words this afternoon are on my behalf.

Did you have fun?

She wants confirmation. She's nodding, in fact, as she questions me, certain that the summer afternoon she planned was, of course, a wonderful time.

I don't know how to tell her differently.

"Yeah! It was fun," I say, looking deeply into her brown

eyes, wanting to fall down inside them and cover my woolly head and my brown body with her soft caramel arms.

I want to tell her they laughed at my hair and my skin and my bathroom towel that wasn't as pretty as the beach towels that the other girls carried. And I am so confused—because these people she has organized for me are supposed to be my friends but I don't feel good with them.

They are everything I am not—rich and yellow and silky. And they are pretty. They will go home in big cars to big houses with big lawns in nice neighborhoods.

They will stand in glass-enclosed showers and wash the chlorine from their milky bodies and silky hair and they will look back at their day at the pool and be at peace.

I will go home to Gaylord Street.

I will lock the bathroom door and peel off my suit and throw off my stupid towel and climb atop the toilet seat to look at myself in the mirror on the medicine cabinet.

The mirror doesn't lie.

I see fear in that mirror, rising from my skin like vapor. And I see truth.

And in 1958, the truth is that I am ugly.

The world says it's so.

I am brown and my hair is woolly.

And I can't change any of that.

How did that make you feel?

A therapist is supposed to ask that question.

But in 1994 I forswear the therapists.

This is self-discovery.

I start mine, not on a doctor's couch, but on a tattered sofa in the den in my house near Denver. The bookshelves there are crammed with "race" books—hundreds of them—bought over the past twenty years by my husband and me.

We expect them to transform us.

But the books are bombs in my hands.

They shatter dumb hope.

They don't teach me tricks to outplay white people—"the tiger at my throat," as Claude McKay, the Harlem Renaissance poet, called his racial adversary. These books—many of them, indeed—barely mention white people.

Most focus instead on blacks.

They cite scary labels—"adaptive inferiority" or "narcissistic damage" or "reactive depression" or "internalized oppression" or "emotionality" or "identity foreclosure" or other bristly terminology—to describe black pathology in response to racism.

I wasn't looking for these labels.

I was looking for blood. For proof. For guarantees by people like Judy Katz, a white researcher and educator, who wrote in her 1978 book, *White Awareness*, that the "race problem" in America isn't a black problem. It "is essentially a white problem in that it is Whites who developed it, perpetuate it, and have the power to resolve it."

But if that's the case—if white people, in their racial prejudice, are suffering, as Katz declared, from a "pervasive form of mental illness"—and if that has "deluded Whites into a false sense of superiority that has left them in a pathological and schizophrenic state"—somebody by now should've come up with a solution for *them.*

But the dusty books in my den are a one-way mirror.

The reflection is nearly always black.

The implication is clear.

The problem isn't white people.
The problem is me.

The problem is *me?*

The dry journals persist.

They force me to look directly at my shortcomings, and own them. And, in truth, if I'm working on me, I've got to study me. I've got to open a book.

I send up a prayer, then I start reading:

"When a group of people is forced for any period of time to accommodate to an inferior status, some form of psychological internalization—usually in the form of accommodative behavior—takes place." These are words from an article on "Ethnic Identity Development" in a counseling journal, written by a woman whose name I don't know—Elsie J. Smith—but written nevertheless with my name all over the pages. I swallow hard.

Lord help me. I'm the darkest on the towel in 1958. I don't understand why that hurts me. Or how to say it. Because it's not polio or cancer or some other fatal physical condition, after all, that afflicts me. But it's lethal just the same. And so confusing. And, as it turns out, this hurt was a crucial turning point.

Smith's words prove it: ". . . ethnicity is a master status that governs the permissible range of the other roles and statuses one can assume."

But what of white people?

". . . many majority group children aren't even aware they belong to an ethnic group . . ."

But colored children? They are aware "as young as four or five that they are negatively regarded in society *because* of their ethnicity."

That's from two researchers, J. S. Phinney and M. J. Rotheram, who I find quoted on the subject of "children's ethnic socialization," a subject that I needed to know when I was a child, but only now discover.

Something bad, indeed, was happening to us when we were children. I just couldn't document it, not like these fancy books with their blessed explanations. But now I keep reading—and smart people emerge from the books and take my hand. Cool scholars climb down from my bookshelves. Batts and Pedersen and Ponterotto and Takaki and Smith and Hacker and Clark. Jenkins and Wilson and Sue and Coles, and . . .

I can't read them all. People of color have been studied within an inch of our very lives, and the reading list seems nearly endless.

We are specimens.

But I can't leave the stuff alone. I am stunned by the material, indeed, surprised that I'm surprised—embarrassed to be learning so late that this "coming to terms" with one's ethnic self, as one writer puts it, is after all such a crucial part of psychosocial growth, but nobody ever acknowledged that in 1958 at the neighborhood swimming pool.

We were just colored kids who talked *all* the time, it seemed, about race and color and its manifestations—hair texture and nostrils and skin color: these "traits" that so intrigued and repelled the world in which we were trying so vainly to fit—but nobody ever explained these matters as "ethnic identity development." Nobody guided our growth through the treacherous waters of "race" with cold, clear facts. So we stumbled.

And we were young, just babies, all of us, feeling hurt and striking out—not knowing, as Smith's words now tell me, that: "A large part of minority children's ethnic identity development entails dealing with this sense of initial rejection of one's ethnic group. . . ."

"[These] situations tend to lead to identify conflict and if left untreated, to eventual maladaptive behavior. . . ."

The dry journals cast a bright light that bores a hole in my skull and illumines my history.

At age nine, indeed, what could I know about "maladaptive behavior" or "ego dystonic" stress?

I only knew that on TV only white things were beautiful— the Breck girl and the Mouseketeers and the Dick Clark dancers. And I knew that white folks in Denver for years wouldn't sell houses east of York Street to black folks. And even now the world and its cities are still coyly divided by race.

So now on TV white people still wash their silky hair and sell shampoo and Tide and ride in Chevy trucks. And in magazines they still pitch perfume that, of course, is called Beautiful. They're still the ideal. The world still watches, and many believe.

So even in China, "round-eye" surgery—called blepharoplasty—is the most popular cosmetic procedure in that country as Asians distort their features trying to look Western. And in the United States, black women spend four times as much on hair and beauty as their white counterparts and, according to the *Guardian*, a London newspaper, "the British market has revealed a similar pattern" among blacks living there.

Some Latinos and Asians are willing to undergo so-called "waif" surgery—to remove fat pads from under their eyes and from their cheeks to look "less ethnic"—although the surgery is considered by some to be risky because it removes natural protection over vital facial nerves.

Brown men with black eyes put green contacts in their eyes to look mulatto.

Black women will spend up to $1,200 for hair extensions that are glued on to simulate naturally long hair.

And skin-lightening cream still sells like hot cakes at a firemen's breakfast.

The problem is me.

In fact I was stupid. I thought I was just my mother's child and growing in 1958. But I was a soldier in a war.

Fighting without weapons. And I lost many battles.

I never enjoyed the "satisfactoriness," as scholar D. J. Levinson put it, of identity *achievement.*

I was engaged in that "delicate quest," to use Harvard theologian Cornel West's exquisite phrase, for my black identity—but my head hit a dead end. No way out. No way up to acceptability.

Now very late in the game I peel the skin off dry words to figure out why. A tiny light shines from the dusty pages, confirming that "self-hate" hardly describes the tyranny for a child in a racialized world.

In fact, I was the bull's-eye in a target.

And I was broken up inside.

The plaster holds now just barely.

The problem is mine.

The antidote is no longer elusive. I know what I must do. I see the solution.

Leave the past behind.

The idea arrives.

It's an ordinary day, after some reading and praying—maybe some crying—when I first discern this notion. Or surely I've heard that tape in my head for years, and I've run from it.

Leave the past? I couldn't form the syllables in my mouth.

The past reminds me that my anger is justified. And my hate is rightfully placed—and *proper.*

But the idea persists:

Just walk away from those memories. Forswear the past—and forgive it.

An audacious idea. Maybe even divine—a holy lunacy. Only God, indeed, could author such a proposal. The idea came in on a heavenly wind, in fact, or as effortlessly. I didn't set out on purpose to find a remedy for the fuss boiling in my heart. I just remember an awareness that I had to fix it or die a slow death.

And both loved ones and strangers, it seemed, were sending me signals that something must change. "This is so angry!" my mother said to me one day, after reading an essay I'd written for a local daily newspaper. She was alarmed by the venom. It triggered a worry in her mother's heart that perhaps her baby was sick. I was. When I started getting letters from complete strangers attacking my bitterness and resentments, those comments felt less like attacks than pleas, such as this one: "Don't you see any hope for blacks and whites in America?"

This was a plaintive question, whose words evinced a clear desire, from blacks and whites alike, for a racial truce. It wasn't just a Rodney King entreaty—"Can't we all just get along?" It was deeper. It was a declaration, rising from the interior of some shared knowledge, that even in America, folks don't have to yield to the "cognitive attitudes" that favor one racial group over the others.

Even here, we can have some sanity and some peace, too—from the things that divide us and confound us.

Instead of the standoff that the races have maintained so zealously for too many centuries, this was a simple and high clarion call for reconciliation.

Old soldiers, tired of fighting, were ready to put down arms—to stop training their weapons at each other's backs. I was one of them. I could feel the sweet possibility of burdens rolling off my shoulders, rushing off my back like a flood of cool, deep water. I didn't have to hate—white people, or black people, or hate myself. Remarkably, I even could love us all if I tried.

The audacity of it fired my imagination.

I saw instinct overcome by reason. And the dead rise up. And the lost saved from our memory plays—the reliving of offense, again and again.

I could even see deliverance if I tried hard.

Or maybe salvation.

But first I saw six little girls at the neighborhood pool, standing half naked in the sun, looking for prey. Old soldiers, we were, in a war teeming with casualties.

Our weapon cut deep. Our words were knives.

You're kind of dark, Patricia.

But the little girls weren't evil—we were just frightened. It was our uncertainty about our lives, our very bodies. And under our masks, we were sweating and itching.

In our discomfort, we lashed out. Poor old soldiers, we guarded our status by denouncing each other, and by even hating ourselves.

Poor sad warriors—we fought a war we could never win.

We needed an absolution. A sweet curative. Something to heal us.

I held it in my hands, and if I'd offered it I could have liberated not just my young friends, but all of us together, but I held back. So now, years later, here I am still trying, struggling to say the words—the magic words—that I've never liked and have yet learned to live. Big magic words. So hard to say.

I must forgive.

Jesus help me.

I must forgive.

Down By the Cross

When you've got too much religion that you can't
mingle with people, that you're afraid of certain people, you've got too much religion.

C. L. Franklin, from a 1955 sermon

It starts in a little church. Forgiveness, for all its moral gloss,
starts on a small pew with chipped paint.

Actually they weren't pews—but rows of leather seats, like
movie theater chairs. My family's church in Denver was started
in 1922 in the front parlor of a woman parishioner's home. Then
in 1935, after several interim sites, the worshipers put together
enough money to buy a refurbished synagogue—bought when
the Jewish congregation moved to a "better" neighborhood.

To furnish the building, the members of the Cleaves Memorial Christian Methodist Episcopal Church held bake sales and
took up special offerings to buy the needed odds and ends. The
movie theater seats, still connected with pewter-toned rivets los-

ing their paint, were a bargain. The men dragged them in and arranged them like pews. Over time, a gold-toned cross was erected on the pulpit. A piano and organ were hauled in. The choir was draped in new robes. And church was in session.

And the Holy Ghost on Sundays came down and the women missionaries wearing white starched dresses were filled with the Spirit and they would whirl in the aisles, some of them, and shout and lose their purses and their little black hats in the heat of that holy passion.

I sat on my chair, next to my mother, watching the spectacle with my sister. Our father was in the choir, singing gospel songs and anthems. Even the slowest number lit the atmosphere. My sister and I knew then what was coming. A missionary sister would throw back her arms, nearly knocking the hat off the saint in the next chair, jump to her feet and take to the aisles, wailing: "Jesus! Thank you, Jesus! THANK YOU, JESUS! THANK YOU, JESUS!"

The ushers, wearing prim black skirts and white blouses, rushed down with handkerchiefs and church fans, gripping the sister by the waist—fanning her, wiping her forehead, holding her arms in control—until things got calm again.

Then after church, these women would again be their same selves—laughing and dispensing hugs and kisses to each other, and to the children. Their faces glowed. They were angels with soft hands and Avon perfume sweetening their necks. Church people: the only black people I knew in Denver who didn't judge by pedigree and skin tone.

So after church they'd go down to the big kitchen on the first floor of the building, put on their aprons, and fry up chicken and stir greens and stringed beans and ham hocks, and frost cakes and spoon out cobblers and make iced tea.

They'd pile food high on the pastor's plate. Then they'd

serve the waiting crowd. Then, finally, we children got our plates and gathered at low tables in kiddy chairs in the fellowship hall and we'd bow our heads and say our grace and we'd eat.

It was *our* food. We ate it without permission or sanction, at ease in our belief that we were in our rightful place.

So it could've been an evil thing, this black church, full of arrogance and self-satisfaction. But deep goodwill and gratitude moved through that little congregation on Sundays, from men and women who—on Mondays—had their dignity trampled before the sun was high in the east.

Maids and cooks and mailmen and school teachers, each paid less than white folks. Each passed over by white folks.

Each believing that—as for faith, hope and love—the greatest of these was love, and love in its full form sprang forth from a man called Jesus.

But Jesus was a white man.

His picture, hanging on a nail in the Sunday school room, was a pastel tribute to a young, white shepherd with long blond hair and blue eyes. A man meant to be loved.

We worshiped Him.

We sang, with complete conviction:

"Oh, how I love Jesus!"

From a toddler, I knew all the songs, all the words.

Jesus loves me this I know,
For the Bible tells me so.
Red and yellow, black and white,
They are precious in His sight.

The Christian message, with all of its fantastic paradoxes, provided our framework for seeing the world: Love your ene-

mies. Do good to those who hate you. Pray for those who perse-
cute you. Do not repay evil with evil.

Trust in Jesus.

Trust in Jesus.

I heard it every Sunday, every week, every year of my life as
a child and, over time, I just believed it. Kneeling at an altar to
"eat His body" and "drink the blood of the new testament"
seemed not only reasonable but desirable. And sweet-smelling
women who fried chicken and served cakes affirmed that.

Trust in Jesus. Ask Him for anything. "Call Him up and tell
Him what you want." The gospel songs directed me.

So at age ten, when I dread getting my hair pressed by a
hairdresser whose technique leaves my scalp feeling scorched—
too sore to touch for days—I go into my bedroom and I kneel by
the bed and ask Jesus to save me from this ordeal.

My mother is on the telephone with the woman, but I'm
praying—eyes squeezed tight, clinging to the bedpost. My
mother finds me there. She looks disappointed. The woman had
a conflict. She can't fit me in. She has to cancel my appointment.

Hallelujah! Trust Jesus. Trust Him all the time. Call Him
up. Any time. *All* the time. He will save you from sickness and
white folks and pressing combs. I believe this.

Indeed, this primal faith called religion is the deepest part of
my black life—the part that I hide, as a child, from white people
because I fear they won't understand it. They'll make fun of it.
And their opinion matters so much during these years.

White people, indeed, seem so rational. So controlled. They
personify civility, with their own quiet hymns sung so neatly and
softly, and their religion's seemingly blithe indifference to black
pain. At the same time, our black expression of that pain is raw
and wild. And transparent. "Help me, Jesus! Help me!"

So, quite naturally, when we invite a white Lutheran pastor and his youth group to our service one Sunday, I am horrified. It's the right thing to do. A good thing. Very decent for those times. But I'm terrified. I'm afraid the Holy Ghost will sweep up the sisters and lay them in the aisles, leave them shouting and wailing and hollering. "Thank you, Jesus! THANK YOU, JESUS!"

All my senses are on alert, knowing the inevitable will soon envelop the room. All my ambivalence about my blackness will be revealed, I believe, by just one sister felled by the Holy Ghost, let alone several unbridled sisters. When one of them suddenly leaps to her feet with a shout and others soon follow, of course, I can't breathe for a moment. I feel betrayed, disclosed. We are now seen raw, naked before white people, and my embarrassment grips me, almost making it hard to draw a good breath. I close my eyes, shutting out the spiritual display—hearing it, but afraid to behold it. When I finally get enough nerve to look over at the white teenagers, to gauge their reaction, it's worse than I imagined. Their eyes are wide as plates, their faces red hot with discomfort, maybe even fear—as they watch the missionary sisters whirling like tops in the aisles and shrieking. "Thank you, Jesus! THANK YOU, JESUS!"

Then the ushers rush down with their fans and handkerchiefs, and the choir won't stop singing. The pianist keeps the pace, pounding out chords, her head thrown back, her mouth wide like a tunnel—shouting her song toward the lights on the ceiling. "He's real! Jesus is so real to me! Yes! HE'S REAL!" The atmosphere has swollen, like a taut balloon, and I expect it to explode, overcoming us all and putting an end to the chaos. But the singing gets even louder, if that's possible. "JESUS IS REAL! SO REAL!" The women's shouting, in response, thus crescendos—and the sound presses against the walls, the ceiling, the stained glass windows, and the carpet and the Sunday school fans, threatening to splinter every ear drum, every window, every inch of plaster-and-wood beams holding up the secondhand building. "THANK YOU, JESUS! JESUS, THANK YOU, MASTER!"

Long minutes pass. And I want to bury myself in the movie seat chair—cover myself up and disappear, hide myself from the scene and from the wide eyes of the white people. Then finally, when it seems we just could vaporize right there from the sweaty tension in the room, the singing slows—down, down it comes—and then it's quieting and then finally it, thankfully, stops.

A queer quiet descends on the room. Only soft moans are coming now from the missionary ladies. The ushers swish their fans slower and slower, wiping one last drop of sweat from one last overheated brow. And I detect one, clear emotion in my gut. I feel betrayed, guilty by association.

Normally the individual dies his own death.

Ralph Ellison, who said that, added, however, that with lynch mobs the victim "is forced to undergo death for all his group."

On this Sunday, as we try to kill off the racial past—acting like it's natural for blacks and whites to worship together in America in the sixties—we are all slowly swinging in the breeze together. Ready for the rope. And, truthfully, I am angry at the attempt. And angry at my embarrassment. Those sisters should've tried harder to hold back that Holy Ghost.

After the church service, during the "refreshment hour" in the fellowship hall, I stand with some friends, arms crossed tightly, avoiding the white teens, who themselves are huddled quietly in another corner of the fellowship hall, looking awkward. I avoid their whispers and their eyes. I am busy drinking lemonade in big gulps. It's wet and sweet, but my tight throat can't get enough. I'm dry as dust. The missionary ladies, smiling now and cheerfully "normal" again, are bringing out gingerbread and different kinds of cake.

They are beautiful again, and I want to hate them—despise them for their display. But they are too beautiful to hate—so lovely I could cry right there. They don't in the least seem self-conscious or ashamed. They had to praise the Lord and they can't apologize. Not even to white people.

They serve the cake.

The business of eating occupies everybody, and that breaks some of the tension in the room. The adults among us have started chatting back and forth, politely—across the races. The white youth leader has even motioned some of his teens to our side of the fellowship hall. And some of the Negro boys, the bolder ones, have struck up awkward conversations with some in the white group.

One of the white boys, groping for his third helping of gingerbread, gets teased by his friends—as he stuffs yet more of the cake into his mouth. But he thinks it's funny too, in the way boys enjoy being disgusting around girls. That starts a round of stories about disgusting things boys do. And now some of the boys from the two groups are actually laughing with each other, chuckling and telling stories, about church camp and youth groups and Sunday worship and school.

Then one of the white boys starts a story:

"One time we went skiing in Winter Park ..." he says, launching into another funny story. At that minute, the Negro children are still smiling at him. But I am struck then, as I believe the other Negro children must be, that none of us has ever been on a pair of skis. Never seen a ski lift up close, with our own eyes, even though we live right here in Colorado. A year or so later when I, in fact, take the ski train to Winter Park with a black teen group from Denver, we are harassed the whole way there and home again. "Go back to Africa! Black monkeys! Bush babies!" White teens, boys mostly, jeered in our faces, taunting our intentions to do a *white* thing like ski, on white snow on white mountains right next to white people. *Go back.* They spat out their rage, even making fun of our clothing—our makeshift ski togs, some of us wore, made up of too many sweaters crowded under street coats and long underwear under old jeans. And, indeed, we must've looked ridiculous to them, trying to appear natural on that cold train, in that strange setting that seemed to belong clearly to them. Some of the black boys, falling to the pressure of the moment, could only answer with their own old rage, screaming it. *Fuck you, white boy. Go to hell. Kiss my black ass.* But their screams seemed kind of pitiful to me, no match for the ownership that the white boys carelessly held over the day. This is our world, they were saying, and we couldn't at that time find a way to deny it.

Yet here we are in church with white people, trying so hard—all of us—to make this coming together work. But it is taking all our efforts, this listening—or half listening now—to stories about the blessed and alien lives of white people, and then trying hard to make sense of the oddly colored lives of ours. If the day isn't a total failure, it is turning out like so many racial encounters built on good intention—mildly unsatisfying. And we've all had just about enough. Even the saintly sisters look a bit weary, their smiles slightly forced now. The smile on my own face feels painted on. My mouth muscles feel tired. And the Negroes that day don't breathe easily until the white people climb in their shiny station wagons and depart for home, leaving us behind with plates to wash and crumbs to sweep and folding chairs to stack together nicely, still smiling, still sweating, still hopeful, still on our side of town.

The book *Buddha's Little Instruction Book* has in it a forgiveness meditation for people who have been hurt or harmed or wounded by others. To use it, you're supposed to "sit comfortable," closing your eyes, breathing "natural and easy." Then while breathing gently "into the area of the heart," let yourself feel "all the barriers that you have erected and the emotions that you have carried because you have not forgiven."

Then, breathing softly, you're supposed to start asking and extending forgiveness, reciting the meditation words:

"There are many ways in which I have been harmed by others, abused or abandoned, knowingly or unknowingly, in thought, word, or deed. Let yourself picture and remember these many ways. Feel the sorrow you have carried from this past, and sense that you can release this burden of pain by extending forgiveness when your heart is ready. Then say to yourself: I now remember the many ways others have hurt or harmed me, wounded me out of fear, pain, confusion, and anger. To the extent that I am ready, I offer them forgiveness. To those who have caused me harm, I offer my forgiveness, I forgive you."

Jesus would put it another way, praying in the dark before he was crucified: "Father, forgive them; for they know not what they do."

The words are part of that Good Friday story, that New Testament plot that we acted out on the stage every Easter in the fellowship hall at the Cleaves Methodist Church. There were white sheets and a crown of thorns and a denying Peter and a Pontius Pilate—actually somebody's big brother dressed in a homemade costume.

I had a part to learn every year. I sat in the dark and watched the rehearsals on stage and heard the last words of the crucified Christ.

I can still see Mr. Cunningham and Mr. Whitney and Mr. Short—brown handsome men dressed in their robes—playing their parts. I hear Mrs. Mildred Hall, my Sunday school teacher, whispering behind the curtain, prompting the forgetful.

I hear the words of Jesus. *Father, forgive them.*

I could reject these words and this plot. But I don't know how. I can't find it in my soul to disinherit my colored religion and its quaint mandates—to love the unlovable, to forgive the despicable. To make peace with white people. To even trust in Jesus.

When I try, during my early twenties, I feel false and unhinged. It takes three words from my Daddy to bring me home. "Open your Bible," he tells me one Monday morning. I am sitting in my parents' living room, newly escaped from an ill-timed marriage—a single parent now, alone. Adrift.

"You need to open your Bible," my Daddy says. He doesn't elaborate. There's no fussing or lectures. In an instant he's gone, leaving the room to get on with his day. The Bible, in its place on my parents' coffee table, is heavy and forbidding. But when I open it, I see the words of my childhood underlined there with my father's black-ink pen.

There is therefore now no condemnation to them which are in Christ Jesus.

I see the words of my history.

And we know that all things work together for good to them that love God.

I see the themes of colored Easter plays and children's choirs and sunny Sunday school rooms with linoleum floors gleaming with wax and scented with Avon-lady perfumes.

Father, forgive them; for they know not what they do.

Through fresh tears, I try to call up the Holy Ghost, that *Spirit of the Living God. Fall fresh on me.* I want to whirl all over that living room, and find myself again—to fasten myself to that force that *stablished* me, as my Daddy's Bible put it, with my maker.

I want to find Jesus.

Call him up, and tell him what you want.

I want to know Jesus because I think in Him I might find answers—a strategy for living inside my brown skin, for coming to terms with white skin, for fixing up my life.

Where does Jesus fit when you're twenty-four and brown and confused? You can't say his name out loud. That means you're crazy. You can't confess him as a savior because his picture is white and, if you love him, you're a traitor. A honky lover. A kook. An oreo Negro stunned by religion, numbed by too much pork fat and gospel singing.

So it takes a deep, deep breath to call on Jesus, to ask Him to show me how to love myself, and my enemies, too.

I keep trying.

At my newspaper job, when a white newspaperman decides he hates me—why I don't know, and I have to work in the same department—I go home at night and fall to my knees. I pray for that man—pray like Isaac, like Jeremiah, pray like Paul and Silas—pray like the white man was my own child.

"Help him, Jesus." There's a white man hurting. Teach me how to love him. Let me greet him with a smile in the morning and send him off with a farewell at night. Doing good to an enemy.

I learned this stuff so well as a child, in my Bible with the white leatherette cover. Praying for an enemy and doing good to him shall "heap coals of fire upon his head, and the Lord shall reward thee."

These coals, according to Sister Mildred Hall, will not burn the enemy. They will *melt the enemy's heart.* Soften him up, so that enemy comes to regard the suppliant with favor.

Of course, that's what happened.

Colored religion doesn't fail much.

The man stopped at my desk one day, stood there a long time, then pulled up a chair.

"Why haven't we gotten along?" he asked.

I don't know, I said. I was breathing gently, into the area of my heart. A soft motion from the chest. Rising to meet him.

It's been a hard winter, he said.

He hated the newspaper. Hated the assignments he was getting, some of them from me. We talked a long time. Talked more every day afterward. The breaths went in and the breaths went out, a little easier each day. And, look, we were now reconciled, or very close to it, and in divine time. Without hard effort. And peaceably, passing all understanding. Is that what God can do? It seemed to be so.

When the man moved back East, and I moved on to another job myself, we shared one letter each—wishing each other well. And once after that, years later, he wrote a long letter and signed it: "My best regards . . ."

I read that letter and I concluded only one thing: This ancient colored God is a mighty God, if I can only believe.

The theologian Thomas Merton, who edited a book of Mahatma Gandhi's teachings, once wrote that those who can't find forgiveness in their hearts are trapped in their belief of "the unforgivableness of sin."

Hitler is the classic example, Merton said.

"It is no accident," Merton wrote, "that Hitler believed firmly in the unforgivableness of sin. This is indeed fundamental to the whole mentality of Nazism with its avidity for final solutions and its concern that all uncertainties be eliminated."

Thus Hitler's world, according to Merton, was built on "the central dogma of the irreversibility of evil."

Hitler could never grant mercy to Jews, because "only the admission of defect and fallibility *in oneself* makes it possible for one to become merciful to others." (Italics mine.)

So in order for me to forgive white people—for seemingly a lifetime of mean actions and hateful laws and unjust tricks—I'd have to first hunt out the flaws in myself?

The gospel language of colored church songs puts it more plainly: "It's me, it's me, it's me, O Lord, standing in the need of prayer. Not my brother, not my sister, but it's me, O Lord, standing in the need of prayer."

Now exactly how many times should a man forgive his offender? "Seven times?" Peter asked Jesus.

Jesus answered this way: "Until seventy times seven."

Or over and over and *over* again.

Love triumphs, Merton wrote, "at least in this life, not by eliminating evil once for all but by resisting and overcoming it anew every day." Because sin isn't going away.

Racial sin will rise up every time. And racial "victims" can vainly try to answer it with sin—its own punishment, as the Catholic saint Thomas Aquinas put it. Certainly, I have sinned in my life by hating white people, especially for their privilege, and hating myself for not having enough of the same thing. And I have been hated by them in return.

This sin must be answered, I see now—for my own sake surely—and answered best perhaps with the crushing weight of forgiveness, freeing, as Aquinas said, the "oppressed and the oppressor together."

That is good colored stuff, no matter who says it. And it feels good to consider, even as I try it anew every day—and often fail at it. But I can try it again the next morning because of something curious:

Forgiveness just isn't a one-time thing.

It's a God thing. And God, as I understand Her, has a long arm and a heart for mercy. God, as I see Him, isn't so stingy as to hold back a second chance. God, indeed, doesn't want to lose us to confusion.

Maybe He's trying to open up heaven for His children. And the colored child in me wants to get there. That little child is still waiting, hoping to be in that number that no man can number, my name in the scroll of remembrance, the Book of Life. Maybe a forgiving heart will unlock the door to glory. Then, in the meantime, ease my mind while I wait for my heavenly home.

Trying to get to heaven. A colored and quaint thing. I won't deny it, not even with white folks watching.

Because time is wasting. And there is work to do.

My colored eyes see signs:

The heavens are ablaze. The sky is burning and Jupiter is on fire, pounded by angry star stuff. The stars are burning and a planet is ablaze and it looks to me like a warning from an impatient God. A sign.

Sings and wonders—what a colored thing to ponder, but I can't apologize. And God is not mocked. And people, white and black and otherwise, know we can't rest while there is so much still undone. There is division to be merged. Indeed, racially there is a universe of trouble to be fixed.

There is work to do.

Consider this: From deep space, the weary Earth looks like a tiny blue dot—our human affairs reduced to a pinprick, our wars and conflicts mere jots in the vastness of heaven.

Surely, on this isolated ball, I can make some peace. My worries over evil history and bad blood and racial consternation can be resolved if I decide it can. Forgiveness, it turns out, indeed, isn't a feeling—it's a *decision*.

The holy people say it best. Here is Nelson Mandela:

"We have forgotten our differences."

Yebo! Yebo! Abba Mandela. Nelson Rolihlahla Mandela:

"We have forgotten our differences."

And there is work to do.

And Gandhi:

"The weak can never forgive. Forgiveness is the attribute of the strong."

And Frantz Fanon:

"I do not have the right to allow myself to bog down . . . to allow myself to be mired in what the past has determined."

And Jesus:

"Be of good cheer, thy sins are forgiven thee."

And there is work to do.

We can forget our differences, Mandela promises. And there is work to do.

And the sun will rise on our efforts.

And the people of God all said amen.

Help me, Jesus. Amen.

CHAPTER FOUR

All Shook Up

Love is or it ain't.
Toni Morrison, Beloved

Then there was sex and I was suddenly and fully eighteen—all bosom and brown eyes and worried and scared. I was petrified, afraid I'd never find love, not the way I needed it. But I dared anyway to let my heart go to none other than a white boy. A red-headed school friend, an American boy—who I'm sure I loved though I couldn't tell him, and who loved me, I believe, but also wouldn't say it. We were just together all the time—"best friends," we called each other. But nothing more was possible. Too much lay between us. My black girl's brown skin. My black father. The white boy's fear of the status quo.

It never would have worked anyway. The differences were so great, the gaps so vast that even an assimilated black girl—

even in the sixties—was something of a freak when white was "normal," and white was good. So in the end I made my choice and I married my kind and, in fact, I exult in *that* uncanny fusion.

But the redheaded white boys, and the rest of their kind, still didn't go away.

At every turn, they were there—with their winks, their secretive smiles, lust written like pain on their shining young faces.

One night in college, after some hours of study in the library, I turned the corner to my dorm when a white boy appeared out of the dark, a phantom clutching notepads and Cliff Notes. "I saw you in the library," he said. "What?" I sputtered, staring into a young, pale face. *"What?!"* I was angry then. I'd obviously been followed several blocks in the dark by a stranger, and if that wasn't creepy—he hadn't had the nerve or the good manners to speak to me in public view, in full light, inside the library building with other people watching.

A few years later, I was at a reunion lunch in Denver with a childhood friend, and our waiter delivered on his silver tray a business card and indicated a nearby table. Seated there were two dark-haired junior executives, not long from being undergraduates, leering and grinning like fraternity boys on a panty raid. I looked at the card. On the back, one of them had written, "Phone number?" I looked at their white faces and I saw history, and I saw cowards.

These white boys—their come-ons were so furtive. Their secret overtures made black women feel like contraband. Like second-rate, cheap goods—good only for lustful intent, only for some secret, kinky alliance.

And we were supposed to be flattered by that.

The effect was insulting and confusing. Because if white

men were the ideal—and American culture said they were—
one of these leering white boys, in romantic terms, must be a
prime "catch."

My sister and I, as young girls, believed that.

We learned it on TV and in movies, where all the sex symbols were white. We cut out their pictures from our movie magazines. In our bedroom on Gaylord Street in Denver—a million
light-years from Hollywood—we grabbed dull scissors and
clipped the faces of the unlikely: Tab Hunter and Paul Newman
and John Derek and other "heartthrobs," teenaged crooners
Frankie Avalon and Paul Anka, and even TV cowboys: Dale
Robertson and Michael Landon and a new star named Clint
Eastwood.

And even the King, Elvis.

Bill Smith's daughters, in the fading winter light of the bedroom we shared as girls, imagined somehow that a man like
Elvis Presley could behold us and see what he would understand
to be lovely and desirable. And at the same time, we imagined
that *only* a man who looked like a Tab Hunter or a Paul
Newman or an Elvis was, in turn, desirable himself.

We didn't know to think otherwise. Black sex didn't have
any faces. The music industry allowed a few. But Sam Cooke
and Jackie Wilson and James Brown all had "conked" hair—
straightened out flat with lye-based grease—and tight pants and
swiveling hips, so they evoked, as such, "the streets."

In Bill Smith's house, street style was bad and wrong. That
is to say it was too close to real—or, maybe, too close to black. Or
too far from the safe, quiet, white "norms" that middle-class
black people so desperately imitate. Young black men, indeed,
in classic fashion were always suspect—even in my black father's eyes.

"What's that boy calling here for?" he would ask.

We couldn't answer. They were boys. That had to mean they wanted something evil and threatening.

And my father hadn't curled up to the sound of a Sam Cooke record. Or slow-danced to James Brown's "Please, Please, Please."

He seemed to distrust the boys who called us—not because they were black, but because they were boys.

That left us to dream. And dreamboats in the fifties were white. Or near white. So Smokey Robinson and Harry Belafonte and a few others—"high yellow" prototypes who, in physical terms at least, were close to the right shade—passed our test.

Kenneth Clark would have a field day with this. When his famous 1952 "doll study" showed that black children preferred white dolls, my sister, Lauretta, and I were replicating the results right in our bedroom.

"He is so fine!" she would say, grabbing the glue and pasting a picture of John Derek in our scrapbook.

"Girl, too fine," I'd agree, pasting Frankie Avalon on the paper—never once recognizing the moment's terrible ironies, or its implications:

Sex was "white."

Falling in love was "white."

Being loved and lovable was "white."

So black men conked their hair.

And chased white girls.

And black girls, in the end, fought sometimes like cats trying to find a place among our men—those who'd love us anyhow. Those boys were dark and lovely and urgent and *present*—and they saved us.

Without them, we would have been left alone to figure out our place and our identity—sexual or otherwise—in a society that apparently believed black females were willing, insatiable sex creatures. But, at the same time, that society called our physical selves ugly.

So when a brown boy named Roger kissed me on the lips, on the front stairs at Cole Junior High in Denver, he was telling me everything I longed to know—but had never been told.

I was lovable.

Nobody ever said that. Not in the "big" world—the "real" world where popular culture decided these things.

Nobody in that land plastered my face on billboards and called me a Breck girl. Or called me beautiful or gorgeous or even sexy, which in America seemed so important.

My sexual self, it seemed, could only be approached on dark streets, through waiters and go-betweens. My physical self, at the same time, was all wrong—in society's bright blue eyes.

But the brown boy named Roger put his hands on my waist and pulled me toward him—close enough to smell me and touch me and see me, but still want me anyhow—and he kissed me.

I didn't close my eyes.

I had to look at this boy.

Maybe he was crazy.

Maybe I was dreaming.

Maybe the warmth from his mouth, his body, his hands would melt my fate. Then I could be pretty.

And lovable.

I could show the world it was wrong about me.

I could erase the lies—drown out the hateful looks and the Amos 'n' Andy laughter and all the other distortions that passed for reality and truth.

Maybe I could change my life.

So I kissed him back.

I opened my mouth and swallowed in his belief that I existed.

The taste was so sweet I could have died from it.

Indeed, I couldn't get enough of it.

I had to have that kiss over and over and over again.

And every one of those kisses from a sweet brown boy erased a little pain. Black girls everywhere know the taste of that relief.

It is water for the dying. And I drank.

I thought it was living water. It wasn't. But at the time it satisfied a longing so deep it couldn't be measured. Simply, I wanted affirmation. I was starving for it. And pretty brown boys stepped up to the plate.

So I tried to forget about the white boys. I stopped cutting out their pictures. In high school, with my white girlfriends, I only pretended to adore the Beatles and all the other shining bright "stars."

But the glow had faded. Or I buried it.

White men, for all their fluffy cuteness, had never even seen my life, and few had bothered to know my name. One might have loved me but he wasn't brave enough. Nor was I. So white men, I decided, were only Evil—all that was ever bad: policemen and principals and policy makers and preachers too.

One told my father to leave his church in Maine. And my Daddy, just visiting while he did an Army reserve hitch in the little town—just trying to find a place to kneel and pray and sing with a hymn or two with saints—turned on his heel and never looked back.

But he never forgot. And after my Daddy told me this episode, I never forgot it either.

Those stories go into the storehouse. And you save them in

your head, even if you don't tell them out loud. But you remember.

So I never forgot that day in city hall when a graying city official, a pink-faced man with thinning hair, grabbed me by the shoulders and tried to kiss me on the mouth. This was during my early newspaper life and he'd asked me to come by his office to say farewell after he learned I was getting a new beat assignment.

And I have faith.

And I believe.

So not even when he closed the door behind us did I suspect anything. But soon enough the graying white man was grabbing at my coat and planting his lips on my face.

I pushed him away with a hard shove. I fumbled for the door. No words were spoken. This silly pantomime—him grabbing stupidly at me, me pushing back at him—took place within the odd silence of only heavy breathing. Mine and his. I was stunned, in fact, wondering if I'd "done" anything to bring this on—then, in the same instant, thinking about the history of white bosses having their way with black women, but denying publicly that they would ever take up with a dark-skinned gal. And with those thoughts, the final push I gave the graying man was resolute, and he gave up the struggle.

When I made it to the door and opened it, then shut it behind me, the noise of the outer office—the secretary answering the phones and the coffee pot hissing and popping and the coming and going of the little suburban city's day-to-day business—that sound hit my ears like a hundred million decibels.

"Oh, Pat!" somebody called to me.

My name trilled across the room. This name—shortened by white people who never asked if it was OK to abbreviate

"Patricia"—rolled over toward me and danced around like something silly, or something cut off. Somebody was being friendly, trying to say good-bye.

I'm a good black girl and I have manners, so I actually turned on my smile and shook hands and made small talk when inside my head I was screaming.

A white man's door sat between my smile and the truth. But, of course, that man never opened it. He stayed inside, certain he was safe from repercussions.

I complied.

When I got back to the city room at the newspaper, where some one hundred men in white shirts and dark ties ran the world—with women so few they could be counted on two hands—I said nothing.

Fear owns the tongue, and I feared white men. They held the reins, and made the rules. They invented the word "no."

So I found an empty desk and I wrote the day's story. Something about a new city policy. Or maybe something about the fire chief. Or maybe it was a city council update.

The grammar was perfect. And the spelling.

But when I saw the newspaper editor by the elevator, I couldn't fall on him and tell him I was hurting. I couldn't even call him yet by his familiar first name. "Mister" was stuck to my lips. He was in charge—as white men tend to be. And I knew that score.

Negroes deferred.

So he boarded the elevator, lost in his busy man's thoughts. And to survive I put him in the category that kept all white boys at arm's length: Enemy.

That worked.

And they played their roles. A white man was always good for some pain.

And here, now in my twenties, were white boys winking and grinning and passing me business cards on a waiter's silver tray. At twenty-three or twenty-four, I was apparently prime bait for these hungry, loveless men. And so were many of my brown women friends.

But it scared me. I didn't know what to do with that kind of attention from the enemy.

"Would you like to see a movie or something this weekend?"

This was 1975. The boy, a classmate in one of my night classes in the graduate school at the University of Colorado, was plain enough and straightforward. An intellectual in khaki jeans and silver jewelry.

But he'd forgotten history. Or he enjoyed the luxury of not remembering. He seemed resigned that I only knew one answer. No thank you.

Later in the car, I rode home with the black man I would marry in one month, and I talked about the weather and the stars and the snow that had started now to fall.

But I couldn't tell him a white man had crossed the blood line, and tried to touch me—tried to shake up my life, not even with a warning.

If I told it, I'd fall in stature in his black man's eyes. I believed, anyway, that he'd wonder what *I'd* done. So I said nothing. I couldn't.

Because I *was* flattered by the attention of the white boy.

This is what we don't admit.

This is what we're scared to tell:

A white suitor conveyed a curious acceptability. It was affirming, *because* of the source. But that was shameful, *because* of the source.

I remember a black friend's pride in her daughter's homecoming date: "He's *white,*" she said, revealing, as such, her *own* excitement. Indeed, this white boy—this benchmark for everything positive—had graced her family in this matter, and she was pleased. She couldn't hide it.

But she also looked ashamed or apologetic. This arrangement had to mean something. Perversion maybe.

Or maybe they were just two kids going to a high school dance.

She didn't trust it.

My own confusion was just as deep.

And confusion is a work of Satan, the Bible says.

A devil, surely, has been at work in these matters.

God alone wouldn't ask a black girl in America to live without love—then when it came, even from a lecherous white man, to be glad about it.

Could I love a white man?

I'm supposed to say no.

I'm supposed to hate these men as if they are ogres. God, let me hate them and loathe them and gouge out their eyes and carve out their hearts from their cold, cold chests.

But after all that, could I love a white man?

I should have. To demystify them, and dull their luster.

I should have lain across a big brass bed and smothered a blond boy in my bosom.

Or at least I should have just held a white boy's hand. That would have killed the demon. He would now walk on clay feet.

A mortal. Nothing to fear. Because even now, the white boys get to me.

I watch them warily.

At a dinner banquet recently, they drank whiskey sours and Coors beer and guided their wives to their corporate tables. They were kings, these men, so they owned things and ran places and controlled, some of them, the lives of thousands.

I recognized a few. Newspaper men and lawyers and businessmen and politicians: men who decide things.

They've debated from a distance such matters as poverty and welfare mothers and government spending.

They think they're liberals.

And they told jokes. They cheered when a football score was announced and their team was winning. Their lives have been good.

America smiled on them when they were young and they took their places at the head of the table and ate.

Even God must now have pity on them.

He must see what we now know:

They weren't magic. They were just human.

"He's so fine," my sister said, pasting a picture of Bobby Darin in the scrapbook. Our hormones surged. But that chemistry was tainted. It was poison.

For a remedy, we should have loved them. And our love might have healed a few, or at least healed ourselves. Love and closeness is funny like that. It cancels, after a time, the falseness of "image." Get close enough to somebody and his or her halo slips—not because they're bad, but because they're mortal. But with white men, I stayed at arm's length—never any closer than "friend." So all their shine, that bright aura around them, stayed intact. Without firsthand exposure to their mortality, I kept alive all that hype that insisted they were special, romantically, more so than other men.

One old taboo kept this pot boiling—the matter of "race mixing." It was so maligned, so forbidden that it made any natural, normal interaction between black and white people in America impossible. In the end, indeed, I had no choice: I had to hate the white boys to save myself, and to hold onto some sanity.

Eldridge Cleaver, writing about this messiness in *Soul on Ice*, summarized his own dilemmas in his poem "To a White Girl." An excerpt:

> *I love you*
> *Because you're white,*
> *Not because you're charming*
> *Or bright . . .*
> *I hate you*
> *Because you're white.*
> *Your white meat*
> *Is nightmare food . . .*
> *Loving you thus*
> *And hating you so,*
> *My heart is torn in two.*
> *Crucified.*

Or, as he says a few pages later: "The price of hating other human beings is loving oneself less."

This was mostly, indeed, about *black* self-hate.

Lord, I hate to admit that. I fear it might give satisfaction to certain white people to hear that some black folks have, indeed, been racked with loathing for who we are. For our color, our features, our hair, our speech. Wanting to fix it all, we reveal that discomfort that announces to the world that we still don't love ourselves. Our *flesh*. Why else spend so much time and money and effort *altering* it?

I must first ask forgiveness of black men for this foolishness. It was indefensible all those years to want them to be black versions of white men. That standard of excellence was warped and ill-placed. It trapped black men into the sin of not being white enough—when white, it turns out, wasn't a necessary ideal.

Black men, indeed, loved me, saved me, courted me, affirmed me, laughed with me, told me it was OK. And I love them like a rock—from my Daddy to my husband to my uncles and cousins and friends. The way they move and talk and look and laugh and be. If they'll forgive me for my stupidity, I'll forgive them for secretly thinking the white girls were better and lovelier, if they ever thought that. Maybe now we can start some peace.

I'll even forgive white men for starting it all. They were wildly and fully wrong, but they refused to see their evil.

Their reasons at first were economic, tied to the almighty dollar.

Howard Zinn, the historian, summarizes it neatly— explaining how early white landowners passed "race-mixing" laws, but not because of a "natural racial repugnance" for blacks. "Sexual attraction was powerful across racial lines," Zinn writes. And wealthy white planters saw trouble—"the potential combination of poor whites and blacks (pooling their interests and genes)."

Nasty ideas grow with fear and greed. And soon the notion of dangerous sexuality in black men and, likewise, the idea of genteel desirability and vulnerability in white women had taken root.

The beliefs would haunt racial and gender politics in America for generations. Every black man ever lynched, with his genitals mutilated, is grim testimony to that awful fact. And every white woman who tolerated brutality from a black man, for fear of being labeled a racist—or from a white man, for fear of being labeled a shrew—is further evidence of this folly.

Black women, meanwhile, remained confounded by it all—mythically sexual but alone, many of us. Alone and confused and waiting.

Love can't abide such chaos. And whatever sex happens in this setting is often tainted and sick.

"A very sick country," as Cleaver put it.

Indeed, many speak and sing of "love" in America, but that love is often blinded.

We cannot see. And every mirror, at every turn, is always cracked. All shook up. Always broken.

Now in the mail I get a letter from a New Zealand native, a white single man living presently in the United States on the East Coast. He is writing to me after reading a short piece of mine published in a national magazine. He has a reply, typed on gray onion skin—a heavy stock adorned with a navy blue stripe along one margin and mailed in a sky-blue envelope. Love is a serious business.

He writes to me of love. He's trying to figure it out.

It seems he'd signed up for a dating service, noting that "although New Zealand is no racial paradise . . . , inter-marriage has never been an issue (two of my five siblings married across racial lines)."

He told the dating service that, racially, he had "no preference." Then something happened.

"Ever since that day, this agency has mailed me several names and phone numbers a month, most of which have turned out to be for middle-class black women in their late twenties or early thirties who are looking to marry a white man! These women are invariably either pretty or stunningly beautiful, quite intelligent, and very well dressed. They tend to be both bold and shy at the same time. Most have been knocked hard by life and have found solace either in church or family. Unfortunately, none has been quite what I wanted, nor I what they sought, so I am still where I started."

He may be sweet, this man. Certainly he is dismayed.

He puts it this way:

"It saddens me to see such wonderful women so unable to find the man that they want and deserve and I have often thought that more inter-marriage would be a wonderful solution. Truly, the issue of race is the damnation of this country."

He signs his letter, "Yours."

Yours 'til winter turns to spring.

Yours 'til April turns to May.

Yours 'til the moon comes over the mountain.

Yours 'til the dungeons shake and our chains fall off, and our eyes that once were blind will surely see.

And then the worried fears and all the lies will once and ever fly away, and finally stay. And color, in the end, just cannot matter.

Then there'll be love. We want some love.

Just need it.

CHAPTER FIVE

A Letter
to
My First White Friend

We have no business, any longer, in being impatient with history.

Wallace Stegner

It goes like this:

Dear Kerry Monroe,

I thought you had a white name. Like Reichert or Feinster or maybe Pritzner. Or maybe Weymeyer. A *white* name.

I was looking for your name—or my memory of your name—when I searched my old high school yearbook. A name like Kuydendohl. Or, at the very least, a plain Jane thing like Knutson.

But then a page turned and there was your picture.

Kerry Monroe. Blond, pretty, smiling. Kerry Monroe like a movie star's name somebody cooked up hot in Hollywood for a starlet.

But you really were a star. You were a cheerleader—I swear it. That was sophomore year. Senior year you were a drum majorette. And nobody, as I recall, thought that was square.

It was 1964 and we were smiling and still hopeful.

So you wore your hair in a flip. You shaved your legs even in junior high, and their pale smoothness inspired me to try my first deliberate act of racial imitation—shaving my legs, using my father's razor stolen off his bathroom shelf, in order to look as smooth and perfect as you: a white girl.

Kerry Monroe.

At fourteen you had boyfriends. They came to your house and sat right in your living room, with your parents' approval. I was awed by this matter-of-fact acceptance of hormones and urgency. It was alien.

But so were you.

You were blonde and, truthfully, pretty. And always so *happy*.

And up close your dazzling brightness—and that perky, bubbly effervescence: like a white champagne that wouldn't go flat—was otherworldly.

TV didn't prepare me for my first white friend.

TV primed me, in fact, to hate anybody who looked anything like you.

But you defied that expectation.

You walked up to me on the playground at Northglenn Junior High School in Northglenn, Colorado—you ignored the nervous stares that the other children were giving me: a newcomer who was *black*, one of only four dark children in a school of several hundred—and you gave me a giggle and a big smile.

"Hi!" you said.

The greeting was terror and pleasure in one instant.

The friendliness disarmed me—but cheered me, because I

was so utterly sorrowful on that first day of ninth grade, knowing instead I should have been happy. I finally was a ninth-grader—an upperclassman in junior high. And I finally looked like it. I'd outgrown a lot of gawky adolescent goofiness. I wore lipstick and stockings every day. I sneaked on mascara. I had real breasts. I had a new, short haircut like one in *Seventeen* magazine.

In Denver, I had good friends—Negroes and "Spanish Americans" and Japanese children whose parents were uprooted and held in Colorado camps during World War II, then later re-settled to Denver. I had black teachers who told me I was "smart," I had a mother who bought me sweater sets and pleated skirts and Capezio leather flats and thought I could do anything.

But I learned that summer that I wasn't invincible. And that things change.

We moved.

My father uprooted us.

The pioneer—my father.

The crusader—my father. Always seeking and striving and going. So he'd left St. Louis a dozen years earlier to take on the West. And at this juncture in Denver, he stopped to look around. The white men he worked with every day were buying new houses in the suburbs for their families. So he would too.

It was an act of love.

That's what brought us to the Denver suburb of North-glenn. My father, God bless him, was trying to do a loving thing. He wanted us to taste the American dream, and I love him now for that effort and the sacrifices it cost him.

But the dream was somebody else's.

Because Northglenn—a warren of modest homes, a kitschy

enclave where, in 1963, a man could buy his family an all-brick, three-bedroom house for $19,000—still didn't have an expectation that we belonged there.

On the contrary, the developer's salesman dug in his heels. He would sell my father a house, but not on the little suburb's prettiest showcase street, Melody Drive. But if my father insisted—and he did; this was a fight now, and his pride and doggedness wouldn't let him abandon it—he could have one of the other lots on one of the streets *near* Melody Drive.

Of course, the salesman was cagey. He offered lots that all had shortcomings—like the lot that was at the end of a very nice street, in the front yard. But the backyard was a fence away from the busiest freeway, the Valley Highway, in the Denver metro area.

Take it or leave it, the salesman said.

At this point, of course, the question of housing—as in shelter; or neighborhood—as in friendly people who live next door—had fallen in priority. My father instead was fighting his own battle.

He would buy the house he wanted in Northglenn, no matter how long it took, on *principle*.

He would leave Gaylord Street.

He would show a white man his resolve.

Lawyers were called. One of them even came to our house on Gaylord Street, sat in our living room, and tried to persuade my father not to force the issue, not to press his client on this particular section of Northglenn. But my father wouldn't back down. Bill Smith was a soldier, and a veteran, after all. He called *his* lawyers. Bluff was called. A deal was cut. On May 27, 1963, at 8:06 A.M., my father signed the mortgage on his three-bedroom, three-bath ranch home—with a partially finished basement and a ten-by-ten concrete patio slab in the backyard. Two blocks from Melody Drive. In Northglenn.

This was victory. I knew it then. I know it now. God help me, it didn't feel like victory.

God help me, indeed, not to dishonor it—because, over time, I grew to love that little home and the warmth and security that my good parents offered there.

But in 1963, I couldn't love it. Or understand it.

Northglenn was land's end.

Northglenn was the sound of "nigger," the first place I heard it directed at me, for me.

A little girl, no more than six, looked up at me riding my bicycle down Melody Drive one day and the word sprang whole without effort from her tiny, pink lips. "You're a nigger," she said, pointing matter-of-factly, then she went back to playing.

There is a shock that paralyzes when that word is spoken, even by a six-year-old. Logic says it shouldn't matter. "Nigger" is just a word. But "nigger" is an accusation. It always requires a response.

That day on Melody Drive, I had to ask myself:

Do I now try to kill this child? Do I beat her half silly and ride off into the sunset satisfied, and justified too?

Instead I rode home to the ranch house, and pushed my bike into the attached double garage and went into the kitchen with the coppertone appliances and I did nothing.

And the nothing got stuck in my throat like a wad of caution:

Don't speak.

Don't say anything to upset the false picture of tranquillity here. Patricia, don't even think about saying something that dishonors your Daddy's efforts to get us out here.

A fourteen-year-old's logic struggles to protect a parent's feelings. So I didn't complain. I only pleaded with my father to let me return to my old neighborhood for school.

It would be nothing, Daddy, for me to ride into the city with you or Mama when you drive to work. To go back to the old neighborhood. Back to my old friends and teachers. Back to my world. Back to my place.

No, Daddy said.

Next day, I walked to the bus stop on the corner. And some of the white children there ran around each other, trying not to stand next to me.

Many wouldn't sit next to me. Or talk to me. Or look at me, except to point and whisper and giggle. The yellow school bus, after all the pickups, would arrive at Northglenn Junior High crowded with children laughing and talking together. And me—sitting alone, or *feeling* alone even if the seat next to me was, remarkably, occupied.

So that first week at the Northglenn school lasted a year in my soul.

The memory dares to be sweet. Children now fight bullets and gangsters to get to a school yard. In the South, children were fighting guardsmen and attack dogs.

I fought only a raw discomfort—and isolation and loneliness so acute that, even now, the memory of it nearly takes my breath away.

I am dismayed that I didn't fight back.

When those four white boys in the lunchroom threw their sliced peaches onto the back of my head, and the sticky juice and the peach flesh clung to the curls that the beauty shop in Denver had so carefully pressed—and when the teacher on duty in the lunchroom just shrugged when I showed him what had happened, and told me I couldn't go to the restroom to clean myself off until the bell rang—I should have fought back.

And when the English teacher ignored my efforts to speak in class—when she watched me raise my hand, the only student ready that moment with the right answer, but she looked right through me and said loudly, "Nobody, I see, has anything ready to say, so we'll move on"—I should've fought back.

And later in high school, when the counseling office assigned me to a "slow" English class—despite my "accelerated" history in Denver city schools—refusing to reassign me until I proved myself "ready," I should have fought back.

Instead, I went home every day—sitting those first weeks again by myself on the yellow school bus—and sat in the kitchen with the coppertone appliances. And I cleaned the tears away before my parents got home from work and asked their question.

How was school today?

The right answer was to say it was OK, so that's what I said. But it was hardly OK. I learned at that school and on its playground and on the school bus every race distortion ever performed by dark people: Smiling when nothing is nice. Laughing when nothing is funny. Agreeing when nothing is agreeable.

So a kind of dishonesty soon surrounded me. I was learning to be false and full of lies—or maybe, indeed, I now *was* a lie.

It didn't help, I'm sure, that this facade—and the pain that went with it—was aided and abetted by my own beloved parents. What was my father thinking?

He would say he was laying claim to his slice of the American pie. A good neighborhood and good schools. And these were good reasons. But the pain of *being* there would be secondary to him.

"Just be friendly. Smile at the kids," he told me. We were sit-

ting in our new kitchen. He had come home from work to find
me, once again, dejected. Stung by rejection.

He glanced through his mail. He sighed. He folded his arms.
I couldn't read his face. Anger? Bemusement? Impatience?

"You'll make friends. It'll take a while," he said.

I tried to show him the obstacles: "Nobody talks to me! Nobody will even sit next to me!"

"Well, sit next to them. Say hello!"

My Daddy, unfazed.

The challenge of an all-white junior high school in an
all-white town, on an all-white street, must have seemed to
him like a minor annoyance, something to swat at like a pesky
fly.

"You'll be fine," he said. "Before you know it, you'll have
plenty of friends. You'll get used to it."

This is how a strong man talks.

He has beaten back fiercer evils. And my father had, indeed,
survived so much: an absent mother, a brutal grandfather, Jim
Crow segregation, World War II, Denver civil servants, Northglenn lawyers.

He couldn't sympathize. I had to be strong.

And destiny was calling.

So play your role, girl. Go face down history and blaze your
trail. In the movies, the heroine would take on the evil white
oppressor and overcome. Lights up. *Fini.*

But on the playground in Northglenn, I only saw fourteen-
year-old kids playing tether ball and "back-combing" each other's bouffant hairdos. And freezing me out those first weeks
with amazing white adolescent proficiency.

Then, Kerry, you walked up.

Maybe you were wearing a flare skirt with a Peter Pan collar on your blouse. Or a Madras plaid jumper. White bobby sox and Keds.

It was prim, at any rate—light-years from what the Negroes and Mexicans in Denver were "styling" in at Cole Junior High.

At Cole, the hallways were promenades with tight skirts gripping rear ends and furry sweaters stretched tight over pointy chests. And boys in men's V-necked sweaters, their gold chains and the cross of Jesus hanging at their pulsing necks.

Cole was noise and heart and heat and color. And double-dare hair styles molded with Dep and grease and bobby pins into gravity-kicking architecture.

And attitude. And Motown. And kissing by the stairs in the back hallway. And after-school socials with slow dancing and cha-cha and warnings from Mr. Genera to stop dancing so *close*.

Cole was heaven. I soaked in the sound and the fury, and I could not get enough. Only the teachers made it even better. They loved us. And they told us.

But in Northglenn, some of the white teachers looked right through me on that first day.

Then all of them changed my name.

"Patty? Patty Smith?" the first-period teacher said, looking down at the enrollment list. He mumbled the next name.

"It's Patricia," I said, raising my hand. His eyes took me in for a millisecond.

"Well, Patty's good—for short," he said, smiling, rather pleased with the idea, ready to move on. (I'm being friendly here, I think he was telling me.)

But I couldn't bear Patty. In the city, that's what old Negroes called white folks—patty or patty cracker. And, besides, that wasn't my name. And it sounded stupid, like something small and broken up.

"It's Patricia," I said again.

He didn't look up. "Well, it's Patty in here."

And it was. And in every class that first day of school in Northglenn, every teacher looked at my name and shortened it.

By lunchtime I was Pat. (Patty, of course, in my first-period class.) And I was alone.

I got my tray and eased into the cafeteria line, watching the other children congeal into wary groups as I approached—but forcing myself to smile, at nobody really, but smile nevertheless. That seemed the right attitude. Look happy.

I found a place to sit, choosing a table with one vacancy. But the children there, most of them boys, got wide-eyed at my nearness—so they scrambled with their lunch trays to another table, laughing, spilling milk and macaroni and hamburgers, laughing as they fled the scary black thing whose name was Pat.

I tried to eat.

The food was dust.

I watched the clock.

Then in the odd way that a gunshot victim can be aware, apparently later, that her lifeblood is oozing from a wounded leg or torso, I felt a cool liquid slither down the back of my neck. I reached instinctively for the back of my head and felt there a clump, a mass—something wet and lumpy and sticky.

Peaches, with the flesh oozing clear syrup, clung to my fingers. I wiped the mess on a napkin, dabbing hard at my hair and my neck. But right away another clump landed softly on the back of my head, followed by the sound of boys laughing.

When I turned, I saw the boys who'd earlier fled my table.

One had a spoon and was launching the peaches through the air. The trajectory, a wobbly arc, delighted the other boys, and they were grabbing their sides, laughing so hard.

Across the room, a teacher stood near the lunch line, talking to some girls. He looked like refuge. Like remedy. But when I reached him, he seemed confused by my story. Peaches? Hair? He shrugged. I was asking to go to the restroom and clean up, but it seemed to him an odd story, a strange request.

"Wait 'til the bell rings," he finally said. Then he asked, "What's your name?"

My name is Pat.

In the bathroom, I pulled paper towels from the dispenser, clanging them wildly out of the holder. I wet them, soaking them with warm water.

But I stopped dead, suddenly realizing:

If I put wet towels on my pressed hair, the curls would "go back"—revert to natural, kinky stuff.

I threw away the wet towels. I pulled out more towels, dry ones, then tried to sop the peach stuff, some of it now half drying, caking, on my head.

Furiously, I was dabbing at my head, my neck—pulling off the peach bits—but, this time, leaving white fuzz from the paper towel on my neck and hair and clothes.

I wet some towels anyway and wiped at portions of my hair, my spirits sinking as the dark hair hung limply from the damp, then very quickly started to puff up and go woolly as it dried. I tried to fold that portion under, but when I released it, the hairs sprang joyfully up.

I would not cry.

No one would see these tears anyway.

But my face in the mirror, staring back at me in the girls' bathroom in a suburban school on the flat plains north of Denver, wore on that September noontime a perfectly crafted look. It was surprise.

On the playground, I kept patting at my hair, trying to hold it down, wanting school this day to be over. I couldn't fully believe that I was here in this white place. Being at this school seemed like somebody else's script, taken off the TV news. This was an "integration" story, but those were historic events that happened in Arkansas or Alabama, places down South where Negroes sang "We Shall Overcome" and got photographed for CBS News, where people talked into microphones and told all the world what was happening and what they were feeling, then they showed their scars.

Nobody with cameras was recording this, documenting this day so I'd have proof that this moment was unfolding and I was reeling from it. I couldn't have explained it anyway.

And then:

"Hi!"

This was you, Kerry, on this day: Perfect blond curls bouncing all over your head. Bright blue eyes. Broad smile. Slight overbite.

"Are you new to the school?" A quiet lisp, but still that smile. Wide as Colorado.

I answered something. Politely probably.

But my mind had stopped working. (Indeed, I posted my worst grades that first year in Northglenn.) But, worse, on this day I had fuzzy hair. A wad of paper towels in my purse. Overwhelming despair that I was here, and not back in northeast Denver with my dark friends—people who looked like me. I could only nod along or mutter whatever I muttered.

You didn't notice. You chattered away. Something had

brought you across the playground, to stand before this new girl called Pat, and you were glowing.

I might have gone blind.

You were a brilliant, shining apparition. So bright—I wanted to hate you, hate anything that looked like you.

But you were saving me. "Those are cute shoes," you were saying, pointing to my new Capezio flats. "What color is that lipstick?" And "Did you like that English teacher?" And "When did you move to Northglenn?"

You had a million questions. A million more things to tell me.

So you weren't running from me, Kerry.

And I wanted to hate that, and hate you. *White girl.* Hate you good.

But you were saving me. And I watched you, talking to me and laughing matter-of-factly on that playground, and I could have knelt down on the ground and held you tight, and let the gratitude wash over me, even while I wanted not to need your human kindness.

At fourteen, I couldn't admit I needed it.

Even now, I'm supposed to dismiss your little niceness. I can even hear in my head, as I did then, the memory of the practiced put-downs:

White girls—they so *phony.*

We did, at Cole, this mimic thing with bouncy speech and a mock flip of the hair. I'm not a good clown, but I would *laugh.* White girls—they so *phony.* That's what we said.

But, Kerry, here's the thing:

After all these years, I have to say it. *Thank you.*

Thank you, Kerry Monroe.

This thing you did was a full thing. A God thing, maybe.

Because you weren't in my face with that fake, nice front—

being-kind-to-a-colored-girl business. You were so matter-of-fact with that brightness that you had.

So I soaked it up. Truthfully, I used you.

Those first weeks, I stuck to you like glue.

Even though I didn't understand you, really. I don't even know now if I really flatly liked you—in the way that real friends like each other. I didn't dislike you, certainly. I was just grateful for you. But gratitude isn't affection.

I used you, Kerry.

I listened to your laughter and sopped it up, needing it so much. I even later on let you ask me questions about my skin and my hair. About my life. "Do Negro girls, you know, think white boys are cute?" You wanted to know that so, if that were so, I could gush with you over the Beach Boys and the Monkees, and the other groups.

But as the weeks passed, and my strangeness wore off and others warmed up and I actually found a circle of people—girlfriends, and even some of the boys—who would sit next to me on the bus, and talk to me in class and eat with me at lunchtime, I sought you out less. I moved on.

Truthfully, I am selfish. I shed myself of you.

Sure, you were always friendly enough, and I tried to be, too—waving hi to you in the lunchroom and in the school halls.

But that initial burst of goodwill we shared—most of it coming from you—faded over time. You were just part of the passing crowd finally. Somebody told me you went to a different school our junior year in high school, but I didn't even miss you. By then, I'd gotten "popular" with some kids—in the way that one black person can get embraced because, alone, there's no threat.

People liked me. That's what they said. I joined clubs. I ran for a class office. I won. I had Capezio shoes for every day of the week. Kerry, I was busy—being black and smiling, making the white folks like me. You were somebody I didn't have time to see.

Senior year, in our yearbook—the 1967 *Trojan Pacemaker*—your neat autograph with a short message written in blue ink occupied a small corner of the inside front cover.

"Pat,

"It has been great knowing you these past four years. Stay as wonderful as you are, and I wish you all the luck in the future. Love & luck, Kerry '67."

Next to the name Kerry, I penciled in your last name. I put it in parentheses—apparently so that years later, if I looked through the book, I would read it and know.

"Do you remember Kerry Monroe?"

I'm on the phone with an old school classmate, a woman named Cathy, who manages a dry cleaners now on Parker Road in Aurora, Colorado. She's forty-five, like me. "I look just like I did in high school," she tells me, and for a minute I don't understand she's joking. But she starts to laugh. So I laugh, too. Middle-aged women sharing a joke. "Yeah," I say. "Me, too."

Cathy and I don't live that far from each other, it turns out, but we haven't seen each other since graduation night.

I lost touch instantly. I never bothered to hold on, save with two nice girls who wrote me sporadic letters, as I did, our first year away at different colleges. But that contact petered out soon. In the years since, I never went to a high school reunion. Never called anybody to get reacquainted. And that airy detachment that I cultivated so finely in Northglenn, with its acres of white faces, I continued into the rest of my life. Call it dislocation. Even now, I stand at arm's length. Reaching out, for me, takes effort.

But I'm calling Cathy today.

I got her number from Northglenn High School. A secretary there says Cathy cochaired the last reunion, the twenty-fifth—a joint party for Northglenn and Thornton high school graduates of 1967—held in 1992. Another classmate, a friendly girl named Eileen, was the cochair. I'm hoping one of them saw Kerry Monroe at the reunion party, or knows how to reach her.

"Kerry Monroe?" I tell Cathy I'm looking for her.

I have something I want to tell her.

"She wasn't at the reunion," Cathy says. "We probably couldn't locate her parents. We couldn't track her down."

That's a shame, I say.

"Who were her friends?" Cathy asks. "Call one of them and find her through them."

Her friends?

"Weren't you her friend?" Cathy is trying to help.

"No." I say. "Not really."

Cathy is chatting warmly now—as if twenty-five years and more hadn't passed between us. As if we were once friends. But her brightness doesn't annoy me today, in the way that white "friendliness" once made me grit my teeth. So much smiling and nodding.

Me, nodding and smiling in return. "Keep smiling!" so many people wrote in my yearbook. "I'll miss your smiling face!" "Keep up that big smile." All in the mouth, rarely in the eyes.

The grin perfected.

She so phony.

Kerry Monroe? Cathy is certain. "I haven't seen her since we graduated."

Some people are dead. That surprised me.

Cathy is ticking off names.

I grab my yearbook and a pen, start writing down names. Later I will look at those names, and match their pictures in the yearbook—people dead now of cancer or Vietnam or accidents; some of them brainy kids or maybe popular, some of them just ordinary citizens of the world—and I will experience an odd feeling of loss. These dead people were hardly folks I knew very well or even cared about, not while they were living. We shared the same odd space for a brief time, by coincidence. We sat in the same classes and cheered the same football team and ate in the same cafeteria. I smiled happily at them, but most times I didn't mean it. But this hypocrisy felt justified—because, all the time, I never fully believed that genuine friendship could happen with most everyday white people. It just took so much effort. Their questions and their stumbling around to say the "right" things just wore me down. And now these particular white people were gone and never would return. Dead, a small battalion of them. I had a chance to know them, but while they were alive I never took the trouble with any of them.

Except one—a funny, lovely boy who drew valentine hearts in my senior class yearbook, next to a sweet message: "Pat, One thing in particular I would like to say is I think you are just beautiful and I think you are real nice to [sic]!"

Whatever happened to him, I asked Cathy.

"It's sad," she said. "He committed suicide."

If I could make magic, Kerry, I would wave a wand and send us all back. To wherever we started, so we could try everything over again.

I would find you.

Then I could give us eyesight that lets us see each other without suspicion, devoid of complication.

Kerry, you would appear as a vision—the white avenging angel, but that would be OK. That's what you were.

So this is an ode to you, I guess. And that's a heresy. Kneeling at a white girl's feet. Feeling gratitude to somebody just for doing what was right.

But I have to do it.

I have to thank you.

For going. For reaching. For risking and trying.

Your effort was pure, and God help me if I can't say that now—and thank you for it, too.

"We are skeptical of kindness so unfailing, sympathy so instant . . . ," the writer Wallace Stegner once said.

He didn't know you but he knew your type, and the nature of your gift.

I'm just understanding it now, that more than your face and your skin and your hair—those things I was supposed to disdain and despise—your kindness was something rare and shining.

Maybe it was like a jewel. But maybe it was better.

Maybe it was gold.

PART TWO

Forgiveness

CHAPTER SIX

Seeking

The harshest winter finds an invincible summer
in us.

Albert Camus

I have power. But for a long time, I didn't know it. Couldn't
fathom it. Dared not dream it.

I was too busy being a victim.

And you get good at that.

There's a cloying sweetness to it, playing the racial martyr
and being angry and indignant. Even when you're not angry
and indignant. It's just expected of you—by the world, and its
assumption that a dark person carries that chip on the shoulder.
Even when you're blessed. Even when the days are slow and
lazy and the paycheck is regular and the air is clean. You're supposed to be angry, and afraid and mistrustful. Supposed to believe you're really not worth much of anything. To perceive that

the troubles of this world are simply your lot, and that white people alone are the cause of it.

That made some sense in 1961. The world's troubles seemed indeed my lot and I was trying, in my own small way, to wage the struggle to dismantle this destiny, and make a new day. For myself.

But my girlfriend, standing outside a downtown Denver department store on a Saturday afternoon, called me silly for trying to play my role. She rolled her eyes. Colored girls can do that. I rolled mine back.

"Yes, we can cross that picket line," she was saying. She wanted a pizza and damn the pickets. They were marching outside the pretty store, protesting its narrow hiring policies— waving their protest signs in the bright, clear air. They looked honorable to me, if I even knew such a word at age eleven. But their queer silence also made them look, to my friend apparently at least, kind of pathetic and sad. Looking like victims.

We watched them awhile, and the longer we stood there the more formidable the pickets appeared, so in the end I couldn't work up enough bravado to cross their line. At my age, I deferred to these adults, even if I didn't understand the details of this boycott. But I sensed something big here—that the courage of these people to picket the shining store was drawn directly from the knowledge that others, in more dangerous places, had done this same thing and more. All I remember is feeling impressed enough with whatever they were doing, or maybe just surprised to see them marching there, that I couldn't cross their barrier. I felt immobilized there on that sidewalk, on 16th Street in downtown Denver.

The pickets had formed a long, oblong circle and were marching in that loop, around and around, slowly and quietly, holding their signs. The men wore suits and hats, the ladies wore Sunday coats over "good" dresses, and high-heel shoes. Their hands were covered in snow white gloves.

They were their own middle passage and trail of tears and salt march, all together at once. Quiet. Just their feet stepping, stepping.

My friend and I kept watching, impatience and itchiness growing. In a few years, we would both be at college wearing Afros and hollering *Black power!*, wondering why the nationalists' catchphrase failed to fully satisfy.

But right now, we wanted pizza and twenty-five-cent Cokes and an hour of aimless strolling through the shiny store.

But I was frozen to the sidewalk. I'd seen too much. Been to Dixie as a small child, sat in the nigger seats in the sweltering balcony of a North Carolina movie theater. I'd dug in the sand on a "colored" beach, waited outside behind the canteen to get "served" dinner in a paper bag through a hole in the wall. No seats inside for colored.

By mistake, I'd put my lips on a "white" water fountain in a downtown department store in Durham, North Carolina. My grandmother snatched me away like the water was white-hot fire. She was nervous for days.

"Are you coming with me or not?" My friend put her hands on her hips, impatient—this Colorado girl, spared life's ugliest indignities.

I impatiently answered back.

"We're not supposed to," I whispered. The conversation seemed illicit. "Well, I'm going in," she said, walking away, but I didn't want to listen. I avoided the eyes of the silent, stepping picketers, turned my back and watched the cars glide by, not able to watch my friend slip through the solemn Negro picket line and disappear, like a fearless brown bird, through the swinging glass door.

I stayed behind, waiting. Maybe I wanted, at this the first truly adult decision of my life, to understand what I'd done.

It wasn't bravery. Or even obedience. My father hadn't forbidden me to cross the picket line downtown. I'm not sure he had even talked to me about the situation.

But there is something primal, Joseph Campbell, the mythologist, would say, that compels you to sacrifice yourself—"losing yourself, giving yourself to some higher end ... we undergo a truly heroic transformation of consciousness."

A primal hero, at eleven? Maybe not fully.

But something small but significant was happening that afternoon, some beginning. Some tiny understanding that the petty store and its stingy rules and narrow ideas were all orchestrated by scarred men who had broken away from the eternal human circle—and their narrow ways demanded a response.

Get their attention. The pickets were doing that.

You couldn't not notice them, and something akin to pride stirred up within me as I watched the silent marchers. Their dignity was palpable, and so was their sense of purpose. This was classic drama performed right before my eyes and they were the main actors. Stepping, marching, silent.

Close your eyes and watch them move.

The "physical grace" of Negroes, Norman Podhoretz, the neoconservative intellectual, once wrote, was something to envy. When a Negro couple moved across a dance floor, or a Negro athlete played baseball or basketball with skill, the sight, said Podhoretz, made him "capable of aching with all my being."

"They are on the kind of terms with their own bodies that

I should like to be on with mine, and for that precious quality they seem blessed to me."

More than a few pundits chastised Podhoretz for this sentiment, written, as it was, for the February 1963 issue of *Commentary*, in which Podhoretz confessed that he otherwise both "hated" and "feared" Negroes—a result of childhood encounters with black bullies in a tough Brooklyn neighborhood. These Negroes in downtown Denver were themselves graceful. But a holy aura, yes, covered them, enveloped them, and they seemed to me both beautiful and almost fearless. I looked at them again, closer this time, dared even to look in their faces. They were handsome and glowing and majestic. Heroic. Marching together in their own silent ballet, choreographed it seemed by God himself. That's the look of self-sufficiency, when one pushes purposefully away from defeat and stands tall, moving toward high ground.

The white racists hated the sight of this bravery. Their reddened faces, captured in news photos of the time, were contorted with rage. They couldn't bear the sight of Negroes not fearing them, or not needing them. That sufficiency nearly disarmed the racists and they clenched their fists and cried out desperately, "Nigger! *Nigger!*"

But heroes don't flinch.

The elegant men and women on the picket line in Denver weren't arousing angry epithets that day, but still they were daring to become their full selves, standing up straight.

Only victims crouch and whimper.

I watched. I needed to see this. This was first-tier protest of a new kind, orchestrated by a warrior named Martin King who preached that Christian love informed by the Gandhian tactic of nonviolence was a *powerful* force and Negroes should use it in their struggle for dignity and for freedom.

Freedom?

This was, too soon, itself a cliché.

It meant the freedom, not only to live, but also the freedom to cry—to linger in one's miseries because, for a while, that felt real good. Almost like a medicine. Indeed, black folks' cries induced guilt in white folks and *that* felt good. So Negroes, as we now called ourselves, got good at crying loud and believing that this expression of our pain was our God-given right, and for our good.

Indeed, our pain inspired our music. And it was wondrous. Pain provoked our humor, and that was cleverly good too. The way we moved our bodies, so fluid and fully inseparable from our experience, was all sublime and beautiful and it came, too, from our suffering. We perhaps, indeed, were one and the same with our ordeal—with its pain and misery and sensuality, its noise and heat and burnished light and darkness. So while Martin King gave us the courage and the permission to try to fix our situation, many of us got stuck instead expressing our pain over it. And why not? Those expressions were vibrant and emotional, musical and tactile. They were the food we ate and the steps we danced and our songs and poems and stories. Blues and jazz and ritual. These expressions, born from our own tribulation, gave us all—trapped, as we were, in North America—our cultural identity. There was danger in letting that go—in not being victims—because, then, who would we be?

Who would sing our blues? Shake and roll our hips and snap our fingers? Throw food on the grills, light the fires and turn the spits? How could we dance? How could we *feel* good?

Hannah Arendt, the late political philosopher and writer, once answered such questions in a long conversation with James Baldwin. Recalling that afternoon in an interview, Baldwin said Arendt told him directly that "the sensuality ... and the

warmth, and the fish fries, and all that—are typical of all oppressed people. And they don't, unluckily, she said—and I think
she's entirely right—survive even five minutes the end of their
oppression."

Victims must know this. Instinctively, we know this. So we
hang on tight to the things that give voice to our pain. We like
the sound of ourselves.

But that Saturday in Denver, the pickets were making up a new
sound. Quiet. They were nearly silent, marching to selfhood,
and in their composure they were announcing their separation
from oppression. Their *rejection* of oppression.

These people were *somebody*.

Part of me ached to understand them, maybe even be like
them, but there was a price to pay. First, ridicule. Even my
girlfriend felt free to shame me for admiring the silent warriors.
"These tired, marchin' people ... I'm not thinkin' about
them. I'm goin' to get some pizza!"

Black nationalists certainly dismissed them, too, of course.
And white separatists disdained them, calling them nigger anar-
chists and uppity traitors. Or just plain calling them bullheaded,
stupid people pursuing a hopeless cause.

The proof, perhaps, was the fact their "victories" seemed
small—a seat at a lunch counter, a public toilet without racial labels, a bed in a motel off a Southern interstate highway.

When the change came and the toilets and the little greasy
cafés and the bus terminals and motels opened up to us, reluc-
tantly, that seemed improbably like victory.

But when my own family finally sat down in Dixie at a
booth in a national-chain restaurant, finally ordered off the
menu from inside—the little window in the back was beyond
my father's tolerance—then finally dipped spoons into the

creamy beautiful yellow ice cream, the shock and the disappointment might have killed us. The white man's ice cream:

Bland. A sad, pathetic, spineless fake-vanilla, fake-yellow
so-called ice cream. Nearly tasteless.

My father, after many moments, said what we all were
thinking. "If this is what white folks been eating all these years,
we haven't missed a thing." He didn't add what we couldn't say,
but still were feeling—a kind of shame for coveting white folks'
goodies. In the end, their little perks didn't seem like much at
all. Just a seat in a cheap restaurant and bad ice cream.

But for some, being a victim still seems better, clearly, compared
to the humiliation of such small "triumphs."

Why otherwise do smart black people hang on to our misery? Crying about bad tables in fancy restaurants, about taxis
that don't stop, about squirrely cops and closed country clubs
and locked minds? I've lodged such gripes myself. Ellis Cose, an
African American journalist, says, rightly, that America "is filled
with attitudes, assumptions, stereotypes and behaviors that make
it virtually impossible for blacks to believe that the nation is serious about its promise of equality—even (perhaps especially)
for those who have been blessed with material success."

That's my situation now, even as it was at age eleven on 16th
Street in Denver.

But that was the wrong worry for me, even then. Because I
already then held something in my hand that exorcises demons
and the little annoyances of life in America—those "seemingly
trivial encounters" that, Cose argues, "are in the end what most
of life is."

What did I possess?

I finally grasped what the quiet Negro pickets held in Denver that Saturday, marching down the street, quietly stepping.

Moving up to glory. Marching to redemption. Such beautiful quiet people, showing me all along what I have always really owned:

Power.

It starts on the inside.

I didn't see that for years—believing instead that power, in the form of the approval of others, came from some place outside of me. I handed over my power, in fact, to others—white folks especially. *Tell me I'm OK. Befriend me, hire me, admire me, give me a good table at your restaurant, sell me a house in your neighborhood, talk to me, listen to me, look at me, love me.*

But white people can't satisfy all these needs—because *nobody* externally can possibly fill up somebody else's internal longings. That inability, of white folks to satisfy my emotional needs, has been part of my *disappointment* with white people. I hated them, indeed, for not filling me up.

So I struck out at them. Viciously, with words. In a bimonthly column I wrote for a local daily newspaper, the *Rocky Mountain News*, I labored for eight months during the early nineties with hate-filled words. I vented my spleen in that column, lashing out at "issues"—but, truthfully, striking out at the "white" demons in my head.

Some of the columns were venom, but pretty, because I sometimes can write "pretty" that way. I dressed up my hate.

But naturally, the response was just as hateful. I got hate mail throughout the short time I wrote the column—a short time because the forum ran out of steam. Hate soon consumes itself, because hate eats up oxygen and other life-giving properties. Hate can't yield anything of worth or value, not for very long anyway.

And, indeed, no matter how loud I hollered, or how hard I

hit in that column, nothing came of it. No lives got changed. No institutions got reformed. No souls got saved. And race, as a topic, still was confounding to me and apparently to my readers as well.

And apparently to my editors, who canceled the column before it ran even a full year. The editorial page editor was nice about it when he telephoned, explaining the newspaper no longer could afford to pay local columnists. My last check would be in the mail. But I believed then, as I do now, that he'd tired of the tirades. I was tired myself. Hate isn't sustaining or affirming, and the column wouldn't regenerate itself.

After a while, I started writing for other publications, but with one important difference. I moderated my voice—because, candidly, I wanted to discourage negative feedback. It stings. Anybody who says hate mail doesn't hurt is numb or lying. I'd had my fill of it. But I still wanted to write about race matters. So I decided to try a softer, more moderate tone, even though I didn't feel moderate. I was just appealing to a higher nature, out of expediency, even before I'd cultivated a higher nature. And the pieces sold well. Editors liked them. During a period in the early nineties, every article on race that I submitted to various national magazines was purchased. And many were reprinted.

Then the miracle:

The response.

Letters tumbled in—from all over the country, including Alaska and Hawaii, and also from the Canadian provinces. It seemed that my "hopeful" pieces—calculated, frankly, to protect me from readers—had me deluged with new readers. Thoughtful people, responding to the softer, more upbeat messages, affirmed my moderation. In droves, they affirmed it.

Professors asked permission to reprint some pieces for their students. Pastors asked to reprint pieces for their congregations. I got "atta-boys" from strangers in high places.

I was amazed and secretly ashamed. I was writing about race, but without the shouting, and also writing with *hope*. This was "nice," my readers told me, a way to address critical race topics without raising hackles. But I was writing out of self-preservation. And decent, honest people were saying the approach was making a difference. It was changing their lives. Ordinary people, especially, were telling me this. And not just about race matters. The forgiveness and conciliatory tone I was dispensing—blithely, admittedly—was prompting people to look at all their relationships. My mail was confirming that.

Like the letter from the state penitentiary in Walla Walla, Washington—six pages, handwritten on narrow-lined notebook paper:

"All my bad days are behind me, and maybe some of my pain will change to joy by putting my arms around my daughter for the first time. . . . My attitude has been transformed. . . . I will never look back on my dismal past. . . ."

Or this letter from West Virginia:

"Your article helped sensitize me to an alternative—be willing to try again, be willing to admit fault, be willing to wear egg to help another save face for the purpose of touching humanity within both myself and my 'neighbor.' Thanks for the prompting."

Or this letter from Des Moines, Iowa, marked "URGENT":

"You see, ours was a mixed-marriage. . . . I guess I got so used to 'walking on eggs,' I sort of tried to get the best out of the worst situation, like just being able to exist at a level of sheer survival. This attitude has led to my downfall and I must get this back into its proper perspective. . . ."

A letter from Cincinnati, Ohio:

"We need to get the young people to understand *just how very important they are* to all of us, our schools, our society and most important to themselves. We cannot afford as a society to have these young people continue to give up and quit. . . ."

From St. Louis:

"As a child growing up, I lived in a rural all white area (a very small farming community). My father and grandfather were both very prejudiced people but my mother, bless her soul, was different. . . ."

From Prospect, New York:

"Your article . . . made me consider my own moments of blundering past moments of opportunity . . . to widen my blinders a bit so that I see just a wee bit more clearly."

From Philadelphia: ". . . your words enabled me to tell them that I was sorry. . . ."

I am sorry.

All the angry words I'd written before had not produced this kind of outpouring—hopeful and healing. I am sorry, indeed, for the hate I spewed into the cosmos because it generated Nothing.

"You must be a wonderful person," a woman wrote from Alton, Illinois. But, no, that's wrong. I'm a charlatan and a coward, too. I just stumbled—thanks to God and His gracious mercy, love, and goodness—onto a solution for my own hate-drenched existence, without for a second even praying for this solution. I just found it by mistake.

I just saw some light.

I saw the power in forgiveness, and the forgiveness in power. By mistake. It was an extraordinary surprise—that, on my own, I could be good. I could be acceptable just by doing an acceptable thing. I could even arouse the higher natures of a few others, inspiring them to see hope and the beauty of reconciliation and to believe in their ability to evoke such healing. That is Power.

And it was like a veil lifting, like scales falling from hardened, hopeless eyes.

I saw forgiveness—as a healing impetus, a soothing balm, a strategy that I could personalize and apply one day at a time, one antagonist at a time, one stinging hurt at a time. And it felt "proactive." Strongly moral. Clearly superior to the stinginess and intractability of the hate I had nurtured so well for so long. Hope and forgiveness? This was high ground. It was radiant, a voluptuously generous love source that warmed the soul and evoked hope—showing me what I could become in racial matters: a catalyst for *good* change—then holding me and squeezing me and schooling me on what I could finally become for myself.

I could be a *human* human being.

CHAPTER SEVEN

Finding

Every once and a while I will come out and tell you
what time of night it is.

Sojourner Truth, 1835

The hard work of forgiveness.

I was ready. But I wasn't 100 percent sure how to proceed.
I was just aware that already something had changed. Something was different.

Gone was that feeling that I had to be angry at somebody,
white people especially, all the time. That anger felt for years
like a duty and a right. To always look for offense. To stay wary
and angry and watchful. To distrust.

All around me now, instead, I saw the world rushing
along—and I looked at the white people in it, and they seemed
so average and ordinary and, for the most part, actually benign.

Like me, they appeared to be coping while struggling—to pay bills, feed and house and rear children, care for spouses and loved ones, keep the car running, the roof patched, the larder stocked, the teeth cleaned, the limbs moving and working and having their being, and the heart beating. Just like me. They were feeble but trying.

I looked at myself more generously now, as well. That is the magic of forgiveness. I was less demanding of myself, not so harsh and self-critical. I was even dressing differently, not "displaying" myself as much in revealing or overpriced or trendy clothes—many of which were either too tight or too uncomfortable, or both—and not judging other people so much on what they were wearing or doing or saying. People just seemed less threatening and less disappointing—white people, certainly, but black people too. Including myself to myself.

I felt a new ease about things that wasn't completely or fully realized in my heart, but a sort of softness had settled on things. Looking out on the world, I perceived that the lights weren't so bright and hot. The itches of life weren't so omnipresent. On many more days, the breathing came easier. My blood pressure was even lower—although it has never been alarmingly high. But during a doctor's visit for a routine checkup, the head nurse in the office who has known me for years even made note of the drop. She read the gauge: 120 over 80. Like a college kid's, she said, teasing me. Some stress was gone. Deep in my bones, and maybe in my heart, it was starting to register.

This was new for me and I contemplated the years I had always felt so angry, always looking for offense. For white people, indeed, I'd kept an antenna tuned—always aware of a certain brashness and confidence that I believed made white people, in general, seem so cold and mean.

I recall a small incident at Denver's former airport, Stapleton International, which as incidents go nevertheless at the time felt big and ugly and *typical*.

I saw a white lady passenger order a black woman to "watch my bags while I get a taxi." The white woman assumed that the black lady was an airport security guard because she was standing, waiting, by the luggage carousel. But the black woman was a traveler, too. She'd been on our plane. I'd noticed her luminous dark skin, admiring its smoothness despite her old age.

But the white woman was oblivious to her. She could order the woman to "watch my bags"—without a backward glance or even a please or a thank-you, and not think twice. This was just a brash instruction from a busy white lady rushing to get on with *her* life. Her life would be important to her—more important existentially, she surely believed, than the life of any old black woman standing in her space.

So I pounced on this moment. I took it on myself to point out to the black woman, who looked confused at first, what the white woman had assumed. "She thinks you're the guard!" I was indignant. I wanted recompense. And an apology. And the whole of history and time to come down on the white woman with her haughty voice and snappy ways, and set her straight.

But then I looked at the black woman's smooth dark face and—this surprised me—she was smiling. She was amused. "Well," she said quietly with a shrug, "I hope she finds her a taxi." Then still smiling, she picked up her suitcase and walked away, into the arms of waiting, happy loved ones, and never looked back.

And as she left I remember seeing a sort of revelation, as if it were painted in neon above her head, with one bright word: choice. The old lady had *chosen* not to bother herself or this moment or her reunion with her happy waiting family with the stupidity of an insensitive stranger.

I could make that choice, pick and choose my moments of racial rage. I could extend and grant forgiveness as I saw fit, but also ask for it.

This was a new way.

This was forgiveness in action, a real-life example of the attitudes I'd built into my writing—but still didn't fully understand or believe, or know how to realize myself.

Racial forgiveness. It was a provocative and an intriguing concept, but how would it work on an everyday basis? Sure I longed to consciously achieve it? But could I fully experience *every day* the racial serenity so evident on the faces of wise, old women? Would I permanently achieve their composure, experience their sheer courage, wear their beautiful, lustrous smiles?

I searched out every piece of information I could find on forgiveness, trying to learn of its nature, of its shape and tone and sound and smell.

What I learned surprised me.

Indeed, it contrasted with what I'd always believed about forgiveness—that it was an instant pardon—snap!—that immediately released the "bad guy" of any responsibility for doing hurt or harm. Or that it overlooked the "bad thing" as if it had never happened.

But that's all wrong. Forgiveness is hardly that at all. It's not simply giving in, or overlooking bad pain.

Indeed, "name your pain." I found that advice in a book called *Forgiving the Unforgivable* by a clinical professor of social work, Beverly Flanigan. I bought the book, and scores of others, looking for guidance, and for answers. Flanigan's sage advice: Call pain what it is. Admit "you are harmed." Examine the injury. Look at the wounds. Study their shapes and contours and their consequences. Then talk about the injury. Tell somebody, maybe even the person who did the hurting. Or maybe tell somebody who's just sympathetic and willing to listen. But confess. Say, hey somebody, this hurt me. This racial weight, hanging so long around my heart, is killing me.

"When you . . . tell your story," wrote Flanigan, "and watch people's responses or listen to their reactions, you . . . begin to understand what your injury meant." That's critical, she said, because "when you forgive someone for injuring you, you should know what the injury is and what it really means for you."

This was clear, plain advice.

So I first asked myself, Who most makes me angry?

White people, certainly. I was angry at their privilege, as I perceived it, because it seemed to happen for them just by being born. Being white, indeed, was a blessed assignment, a holy membership—or appeared to be. And I resented that, especially the ease that being white meant over being anything else in my culture. It meant being OK, by accident of birth. Being black or brown—or anything else than white—meant the opposite. That's how I understood this, and I hated the meaning of this understanding. So I hated white people in general, although individual whites had become my friends in various settings. But the group I held in contempt. "They" were a negative force and they personified everything that had stood in my way—for me as an individual and as a member of my own group.

White people! They were Enemy. They were rival and adversary and pain and hurt—a constant, exhaustive irritation. With their haughty, put-down looks, their indifference, their suspicion, their nervous fear when they encountered dark people—grabbing at their purse straps in their elevators, following us around coyly in their department stores, spoofing us in their movies, cheating us, scorning us, then ignoring us. My rage about these things seemed reasonable. And natural. And inevitable.

The attitude of supremacy, indeed, seemed to fuel their very existence. It colored every interaction—anointing them, cursing everybody else. So there were always the insults. And cool, blithe assumptions about dark people—that we weren't as smart, as virtuous, as clean, as lovely, as brave, as chosen, as acceptable as white people.

Then there was my father. He was in this picture, too. But that didn't make sense. Here was a good, fine, golden man. A good provider and a steady, moral presence—a man who taught me the Scriptures and the Apostles' Creed and his own creed. A college graduate, indeed, who would've finished a master's degree had he not gone off to fight in that good war. A civilian accountant who traveled the world for the Air Force, working round the clock for Uncle Sam even if Uncle Sam wouldn't always work for him and his. A proud man, indeed, my Daddy. A lieutenant colonel in the U.S. Army Reserves, ready to fight at a moment's notice for his country, for his God, for his family. A man, indeed, who brought home to his children good and solid things—*Life* and *Ebony* and *National Geographic* and a complete set of the *Encyclopaedia Britannica*, and solid pretty furniture to recline on when we read them—a man who paid for orthodontia and college tuitions and summer vacations and countless other blessings, then preached to his girls all the lessons about surviving in America. Rules about always being better than the white people, so they couldn't find anything wrong with you even if they tried hard. So I tried to pass his tests. God bless me, I did everything I thought would please him—worked harder, studied longer, talked better, walked taller. But it always seemed he wanted me to *be* more. Or maybe he thought I was OK, but he just didn't know how to show it. Instead, the critical eye was so often in focus, finding fault—or finding yet more room for yet more improvement.

So over time I grew to hate that part of him that demanded so much of me, but never quite seemed appeased. Hate? Well, I hated that impulse, that motivation for asking so much. For needing such perfection from his daughters—an impossible objective—and needing it seemingly to appease such an imperfect world. A world of fancy Negroes and judgmental white people. Look good and be good and smell good for them. Don't do any of these things for yourself. That was the unspoken message. And I hated it, so didn't that mean that I hated its source?

But where does a black girl go with such a question? Black children in my day honored our parents. Didn't dare spit out protests at these warriors who were fighting every day. We could only imagine what they endured out there in the world. Knew it must be humiliating. Understood it made their stomachs churn, their blood boil.

Why else did Daddy mutter under his breath so much of the time?

I'd pretend not to notice. Spare him the embarrassment.

I just kept out of his way. Jumped slightly when his car door slammed, the sign he was home. Stopped quickly whatever I was doing when he arrived, when I heard his footsteps crunch on the walkway alongside the house. Knew within seconds he'd unlock the big brown front door.

"Daddy's coming!"

Two words shouldn't make the heart leap.

But I always stood, straight up, from the jolt. Ready to, what?—flee, fight, blurt out some pathetic defense for whatever wrong thing I was doing at the moment. Especially if it was fun or lazy or silly. If it was TV or fast music or twisty dancing or finger snapping.

His stern look, scrutinizing, upbraided me, a look that, in truth, probably said more about the world outside than the life inside our home. To deflect it, I'd grab a book, a broom, a dust rag, a dishrag—any sure sign of industry, of productivity. That would make me OK, for now. But just *being* there—it didn't seem to be enough.

A little girl wants to be enough for her father. Really, she wants her father to love her, just for the fact that she's alive. I wanted my father to love me—I had to believe he did, and I surely did believe it then—but, of course, he never told me the words. Never just held me in his arms and said you're mine and I'm proud of you and, girl, I just love you, chile. His style was to *show* his love, and certainly he did that by being there—sticking with his family, never forgetting apparently what it felt like not to have a daddy around. But the words! In the beginning was the Word and the Word was with God and the Word was God. And those little words would've been so godly: I love you, girl— just the way you are. Because when the world says you aren't lovable, and your father doesn't say you are either, a girl has to go on what she does hear. And what my father often did tell me made it clear I was flawed—just never quite right. Walk straighter. Talk clearer. Sit quieter. Be nicer. Be cleaner. Smile brighter.

That's what *he* was told growing up, of course. But I didn't know that then.

I heard his commands as problems not with his past or the world but with me. Internalized all of it. The demands, indeed, left me feeling perpetually dissatisfied with myself. The discomfort I felt in my own skin—this dark wrapping with all of its *meanings* was like a shroud. And I couldn't shed the wrapping. So quite naturally, in the end I was clearly angry at my father— God help me—and my anger scared me, and alarmed close relatives, who implied that such anger was scandalous and misplaced.

I was blaming him, unjustifiably, said one of them.

So, in the end, it was clear again that these feelings were bad and also they were my problem—a conclusion that seemed so logical. Who else, at bottom, could be at fault? For not knowing how to fix all the many things that seemed to be wrong with me. For not being brave enough to express the resentment I felt for having to "fix" myself for a white world in the first place. Indeed, for not knowing how to talk about these things. Certainly, I never told my father any of these feelings. I always feared his disapproval. And I was too weak to dismiss his expectations, too cowardly to tell him sometimes to lighten up. Indeed, not able to laugh at myself. Or even to like myself much. And not knowing this, not knowing much therefore about how to like other folks either.

The problem was me.

Forgiveness would help me recover. It would bring me back to myself, and back to my beloved father—who, I finally understand now, after all these long years, was only trying to toughen me up, to get me ready for that harsh white spotlight because he knew it would burn, understood it would never find me fully acceptable. So he would push me beyond acceptable, because that's how far he was pushed. And that's what some dark people still find ourselves doing to both ourselves and our children, which of course is a trap—just one of many fashioned by that cunning deception called race.

Race! A mighty villain.

Race will even make a daughter doubt a good father, twist her eyes so she sees only what look like flaws, but never sees his beauty—so she expects from him the perfection that she resented him demanding of her. So each looks to the other like a problem—when the real problem is the appalling pressure of race, that beast that prowls around, with lips wet with the anticipation of the kill. Snapping and worrying and confounding and sometimes even devouring the innocent and the unwary in steady pieces, until they're all used up. Thoroughly confused and consumed. That's what "race" will do.

So maybe this solution, this forgiveness, would finally save me, then liberate me—from the need to have to "measure up," but also from the need to make white people pay for all the bad things. My self-doubt. My ruinous perceptions of my family, my father, my life, myself—that paranoia about my color, that it was at the heart of all pain. So I wanted white people to pay, but white people couldn't pay—not all of them, for everything.

I had generalized the debt and applied it to all white people, foolishly. No wonder I was enraged all the time. Living in America, surrounded by white people, I had forgotten as James Baldwin said, the "law," as he put it, "that if I hate white people I have to hate black people." But that kind of hatred is too costly.

It's worse probably, however, to hate some things about your own father. Especially when he's a saint. Especially when the Bible says honor your mother and your father, "so that you may live long and that it may go well with you in the land the Lord your God is giving you."

And I don't want to die. I want to live long and make peace with him and release him—indeed, to forgive him, if that's even the proper response, for these things he couldn't have foreseen.

To tell him it's OK. That I understand now. He was only doing what he knew how to do. Oh, to tell him that I love him. I never told him that, either.

Our tongues were tied.

And white folks, I believed, fixed the knots, then yanked them. Tight.

To ease this rage, this awful confusion, stop the hate meant first to forgive us all. But some of the formulas I read in books—self-help, psychology, devotional—just weren't adequate for racial dilemmas. One author even argued that forgiveness was "simply" a matter of deciding to forget. But there was nothing at all simple about forgetting the past. It felt immensely complicated, overwhelmingly difficult and frightening—like I'd be giving in if I did forgive the stain of race on my soul, and if I then went on to forget it. Another writer suggested that forgiveness shouldn't start until one felt "ready." But is anybody ever fully ready to forgive? I don't think so. But I could, indeed, understand what Barbara Flanigan meant when she bravely said: "Forgiveness is the process of giving yourself and the person who injured you a gift of freedom."

Toni Morrison, the warrior writer, said it perhaps even better: "If you're going to hold someone down you're going to have to hold onto the other end of the chain."

But how could a brown-skinned girl cut her chains, retreat from her history and start anew? Especially when she still believed that her effort had to be 100 percent perfect, or else it wasn't worth anything.

I decided instead to borrow a point from Colorado writer Clarisa Pinkola Estés, a *cantadora* storyteller, who has challenged the false notion that "forgiveness has to be a 100 percent proposition"—all or nothing.

Estés, in her mystical book, *Women Who Run with the Wolves*, argues otherwise:

The person "who can work up a good 95 percent forgiveness of someone or something tragic and damaging almost qualifies for beatification, if not sainthood. If she is 75 percent forgiving and 25 percent 'I don't know if I ever can forgive fully, and I don't even know if I want to,' that is more the norm. But 60 percent forgiveness accompanied by 40 percent 'I don't know, and I'm not sure, and I'm still working on it,' is definitely fine."

This math made sense. It added up. It was liberating, a refreshing argument—which I quickly embraced—because it allows degrees of forgiveness, at the outset especially. Or as Estés put it: ". . . the rest will come in time, in small increments. The important part of forgiveness is to *begin and to continue* [italics hers]. The finishing of it all is a life work. You have the rest of your life to work at the lesser percentage."

The rest of my life. That sounded long enough, or at least it sounded like my conversion to forgiveness didn't have to happen all at once, not even right this minute or at least today. This was relief and permission all in one dose. Then the icing on the cake:

"You are not bad if you do not forgive easily. You are not a saint if you do."

But it's hard work.

"That hard work of forgiveness." That's C. S. Lewis's phrase.

I was trying to live it, on a daily basis—smiling at surly store clerks, ignoring insensitive comments, thinking good memories about my childhood (and indeed there were many more good memories once I chose to focus on them), and even doing nice things for myself. Over time, not surprisingly, I was experiencing less hostility and coldness from my fellow life travelers.

But I still felt incomplete in this work, experimental and flawed. Like a pretender. I was mucking around in something true and golden, but my efforts felt insincere and inconsistent. And small.

God help me.

I prayed the prayer that started this sojourn.

God help me.

I liked the sound of this prayer. It reminded me that something bigger than me would enlighten this process.

God help me.

A beautiful prayer. I prayed it daily. Upon awakening. At the end of long days. Maybe even as I slept. I breathed this prayer, entreating divine powers. Blatantly, I just asked. God help me to find this way, to walk this path. Even when it's hard. God help me. Even when it's vicious. When the hate mail comes from Grand Rapids, Michigan, and Chicago, Illinois, and Phoenix, Arizona, and Harrisburg, Pennsylvania—"you are a nigger and will never be nothing but a nigger"—and when the cold, suspicious stares follow me down American streets and into American stores and across American highways. God help me to forgive other people's fears. Help me to understand other people's suspicions, not to mention my own. Help me to speak compassion to the malevolent, grant understanding to the hateful, give charity to the spiteful, healing to the hurting, love to the loveless.

God help me.

To understand my father's pain and fears. To see that he and his generation, white and black alike, were working with a flawed script, but it was the only one they knew. And my generation, black and white alike, with our flawed reactions, have taken those cues and done our own harm—as citizens, as sons and daughters, even as parents ourselves. Help me to see that by definition a parent isn't perfect. A guardian is only given charge over an infant and expected to make something of her. My father took his job seriously, in a hostile world, and some might even say he succeeded. I'm not a criminal, or not even a fool. But what more could I be—any of us, indeed—if the terror of racial pressure had not so harshly formed us?

God help me.

I can't do this thing without you, Lord.

There's too much history and reason and precedence for hanging onto the past—for clinging to the sweetness of hurt.

So help me to find the world's wisdom on forgiveness, to round it up and learn its ways and wear it around me like an anointed blessing. Help me first, as this expert Flanigan instructs, to "name" my injury—to point at racial assault and call it all the awful things it is: a murder of the soul, an attack on hope and faith. A spiritual rip-off.

Help me to see, as others have, that forgiveness isn't a contract with somebody. It doesn't have to take both parties. It only takes *my* willingness. God help me to be willing to forgive.

Help me, indeed, to honor the belief, an ancient Jewish philosophy, as I understand it, that wounds and pain actually have a sacred quality—and that the purpose of wounds, in turn, is to call forth a sacred gift or sacred calling. Flanigan calls this "claiming the injury"—or recognizing "any good that may trickle out of the pain you are enduring." She is saying, incredibly, that there is *good* in pain. But even in racial hurt?

God help me. As hard as it is to confess, I can admit some good things: Racial hurt has given me a creative agenda that I've explored in satisfying and, I hope, salient ways. And, in that study, I have learned how to see other people fully, not just as caricatures. I've grown to even consider the concept of forgiveness as viable. The victim, indeed, can teach the offender.

God help me.

God?

God surely would help me? Surely—I believed so. But, truthfully, I was angry at God anyway.

Angry at *God*. For seeming to allow "nigger status" for dark people. For giving us physical features that people ridiculed, so we grew to hate those features in ourselves and in each other. For letting the world walk on our backs and spit on us. Spit was hanging from the hems of schoolchildren's clothes when they tried to integrate public schools down South, walking those gauntlets of angry white men hawking their sputum at self-possessed young children—while those brown girls and boys tried to ignore the taunts and the screams and the nasty mess aimed at their paths.

I wanted to rail at God for these things. For Emmett Till's sad murder and for Medgar Evers's assassination and for the No Colored signs down South and the White Only hypocrisy up North. Holler up to heaven with my fists balled up. But my arm's too short to box with God, which must be a good thing because this was one fight that I couldn't win. For one thing, my vision was off, my perspective all wrong. Like that old disciple Paul, I was seeing only through "a glass darkly"—like "a poor reflection as in a mirror," as it says in the First Book of Corinthians. But one day, it goes on, "we shall see face to face." Face to face, one day, I vowed to talk to God, to dare ask Him to explain in full all these matters. All the reasons for injury to dark folks. Surely, He would provide an overwhelming reason. An amazing reason.

Or surely I am wrong. And God's answer will come instead

in that manner in which He spoke to Job—that perfect man who actually dared out loud to wonder why God would allow him to suffer. But God's voice, thundering out of the Old Testament books, replying to Job, also replied to me—not with an answer, but with a question, asked bluntly with a clarity heard indeed only from God. That question goes like this:

"Where were you when I laid the foundation of the world? . . . Who marked off its dimensions? . . . Who stretched a measuring line across it? . . . or who laid its cornerstone— while the morning stars sang together and all the angels shouted for joy?"

God, indeed, making it plain, turned my questions on themselves in the form of *His* questions:

"Have you ever given orders to the morning, or shown the dawn its place . . . ? Have you entered the storehouses of the snow . . . ?"

And still asking:

"Does the rain have a father? . . . Can you bring forth the constellations in their seasons . . . ? Can you raise your voice to the clouds and cover yourself with a flood . . . ?"

God, indeed, looking down on Job, deigned to look down even on me to ask the same blistering query:

"Will the one who contends with the Almighty correct Him? Let him who accuses God answer him!"

It's in a black church on a hot Sunday summer morning when I hear a preacher recount this timeless story of Job, repeat yet another time Job's quavering answer:

"I am unworthy . . . I put my hand over my mouth . . . Surely I spoke of things I did not understand, things too wonderful for me to know."

Job is repentent and, suddenly and necessarily, so am I.

Certainly, as the choir sings and shouts and the sisters rock their heads to the music, I finally see—after months, indeed years of worrying about these matters—that for *me* this issue of forgiveness is first about making peace with God.

That's my little Christian colored woman's matter. Somebody else might reconcile these things differently. But by daring to question not only my father but my God as well, I slowly start to see some things.

First, God never promised me life without sorrow. Racial pain may be the lot of dark people, but God doesn't have to explain it. I just have to trust the Lord to direct me through it. I realize, finally, that God never expected me to be perfect. Man did. And woman. And white folks. And black folks. The world did. But all the while, the Lord was saying, "Child, you're OK with me. Being perfect is My business. *Being* is yours."

Every child born is supposed to know this thing—that he or she is just fine, by virtue of just being alive and *here*. But too early, we start learning otherwise—learning this sometimes from otherwise good people. So the doubts set in, and the fears. And our true condition is lost to us.

Hurtful people suffer from the same confusion. That's why they strike out and damage even the ones they love. Their mirror is distorted, too. What a pity. How sad for them . . .

Sadness for the injurer?

That's what a person feels when forgiveness kicks in. Estés, the *cantadora,* describes it this way:

"You tend to feel sorry over the circumstance instead of rage, you tend to feel sorry for the person rather than angry with him. . . . You understand the suffering that drove the offense to begin with. . . . You are not waiting for anything. . . . You are free to go. . . ."

I'm feeling that now—not anger now, but sadness for my

beloved Daddy, because, it turns out, he wasn't cold or wrong when he demanded so much of me. He was wounded, I see now, from what he missed first as a child. His bleak early life in Mississippi, deep in the South—deep in Jim Crow's season—was certainly a kind of prison sentence. He escaped with his body, but maybe not fully his heart. That wasn't his fault. And I can't blame him. But Jim Crow's shadow is long, and everything that fell under it got damaged.

So the white people were flawed, certainly too, and I feel sad for them. Look what they missed. The truth, most of all.

They really were "imprisoned and enthralled," as W. E. B. Du Bois so aptly put it, by the *fantasy* of superiority and entitlement. Too many white people thought they were special and enlightened or secretly wondered why they weren't. Too many didn't question that dark people couldn't be. And that thinking left all of us trapped in our hate and in our fates.

The price we've paid is measured in big things—lost joy and unrealized understanding, and in our stupid refusal to see each other's beauty, or to detect each other's goodness and potential.

Love, surely, would have been the better way.

Thus, when Mahatma Gandhi—when asked by a reporter how he convinced a *third* of a billion people to rebel against British rule nonviolently, could only give the perfect answer:

"By love and truth," Gandhi said. Then he added, "In the long run, no force can prevail against them."

Love never fails.

Love your enemy.

Forgive one another. Or this, says Estés: "There's a lot to be said for pinning things to the earth." So they don't follow us around. "There is a lot to be said for laying them to rest."

Perfect people can't do that.

But God's not asking me to be perfect, just to be obedient, to follow His admonition to *begin* the process of forgiveness. Jesus told Peter he should forgive his offender "seventy times seven." Over and over again. Keep on forgiving because it's not going to happen at once, nor will it happen once and for all. So just start the process, and *keep on it.*

I start it by thinking hard about my own childhood that, for years, I thought was so unkind, so unjust. Remarkably, inside the bubble of forgiveness it looks less evil—hardly even sinister. The good parts start to rise up and crowd out the sad—because it's all behind me, anyway. And whatever happened, or didn't happen, can all be repaired when I choose to look forward, not backward. And this turning will happen as I'm able, little by little, some days turning better than others, but turning nevertheless *forward.*

That's the only direction, in the end, that matters. And the ancestors won't mind. They don't want us hanging around their sepulchres, sobbing and spitting and moaning about what *was.* "Why seek ye the living among the dead?" those angels asked Jesus' grieving disciples, gathered at his empty tomb. *He is not here.* Or, as Mandela so wisely put it: "What has happened has happened." That was then. And now is now. And Emmett Till and Medgar Evers and Martin and Malcolm and the four little girls in the Birmingham church want us to move on. To honor the sacrifice of their lives and make it a gain. To become all those things the martyrs didn't have a chance to be. White folks and black folks alike are indebted, and we must bury our paralyzing anxieties about race—worries that somebody else is getting ahead faster, or that somebody's racial sin demands somebody else's heated revenge. It's time, instead, to start living up to our collective and individual potential as a blessed human community. We *must* start making connections, not just by race or age or gender or in other affiliate ways, but by linking our talents and energy, our resources, our ideas, our hopes—so we can finally, blessedly, banish our fears. Indeed, we must start *loving* so we can start *living*. And the past? It is over.

If this was some knowledge that I was supposed to uncover for myself, even if it took me years to see, it was worth the wait and the worry to finally discover it. *Don't go back.* Just keep straining, stretching, moving, going face-first ahead—into the winds, but sometimes with them at my back. Pushed along, and sometimes pulling.

I contemplate these things, indeed, and I suddenly and remarkably understand that I won't move ahead perfectly, nor forgive perfectly, nor will I love perfectly. Nor will I achieve these things all at once. Forgiveness, if it's anything, is a *process*. It unfolds as we allow it, and as we are ready.

So I will pray and I will try. And God's gonna love me anyhow. *God* loves me. And God will help me.

Oh, thank you Lord. Praise you, Father. Help me, Mother. Now bless you, Daddy.

I'm on my way.

CHAPTER EIGHT

Knowing

But the meek shall inherit the earth; and shall delight
themselves in the abundance of peace.

Psalm 37:11

A little brown man will lead me.

Mahatma Gandhi, the author of nonviolence—the father of
love and forgiveness for the loveless twentieth century—will, of
course, be my guide to the higher altars of forgiveness. And at
his right hand—none other than Martin Luther King. They'll
teach me the hardest lesson of all: how to deal with institutional
racism and injustice, not just the personal and the petty and the
familial worries and insults.

But at my suburban branch library, the young librarian
stumbles over the Indian guru's name.

"Maha . . . ? Gandhi . . . ? Could you spell it?"

She is young and smiling. I smile back at her over the telephone, trying to be encouraging, understanding that it might be hard to find some interest in this name that's vaguely familiar—but a name, nevertheless, that both of us need to know.

After a few moments, she finds the reference, gives me a call number, and tells me the book is on the shelves. She sounds ready to hang up. But I have to challenge her again.

"Also, do you have Martin Luther King's book, *Why We Can't Wait?* With his 'Letter from Birmingham Jail.' It's in the book, *Why We Can't Wait.* Do you have that book on your shelves?"

Her smile fades a bit. I can feel the light go off. That title, thirty years after it was published, still can make a young girl catch her breath. I hear that catching sound now, almost as if her breathing has stopped for millisecond, then a long sigh escaping her lips.

I'm put on hold, waiting. She returns eventually, and tells me somebody is looking in a book of speeches, which momentarily sounds like a smart idea. But of course:

"It's not a speech," I tell her. "It's a letter."

He wrote so much. I want to tell her that—he didn't just give speeches. Both King and Gandhi—Mahatma, meaning "great soul," a name conferred on the little brown man because his birth name, Mohandas, wasn't large enough for his spirit—these two, they wrote between them surely millions of words in sermons and articles and books, letters and memos and essays, and in urgent pleas. Not just speeches.

Do you have their writings?

The request often ends with a shuffling of papers and cleared throats. And with that long, deep sigh.

They turn to dust, our heroes. Then we forget who they are.

The devil wants it that way. Satan, as some of us still call the thing called Evil, is hustling to make us forget—fuming and pounding and sweating, persuading us to recall the two revolutionaries as just nice little men who preached *harmony,* and other sweet little things. Like peace. And love and hope. So sweet and nice, their little agendas. Hardly worth more than a thought, or a few words on a poster: "The Dream Is Alive!"

But Satan is a liar. And a conjurer, too. That's what the gospel song says. So I try to look through that ruse, believing that something rich will emerge from my hunt for the two brown saviors.

But first I find the mundane.

Martin Luther King was a short guy.

"... somewhat below what is called average height, he is sturdily built, but is not quite as heavy or as stocky as he had seemed to me at first."

That is James Baldwin, writing in 1961 for *Harper's* magazine.

Baldwin, who loved King maybe more than a brother—who sixteen years after King's death said the killing still depressed him so much "I can't even talk about it. I didn't know how to continue, didn't see my way clear"—spoke yet about this ordinary matter, their first meeting, and his surprise at the small stature of the civil rights movement's biggest "star". Said Baldwin:

"I remember feeling, rather as though he were a younger, much-loved, and menaced brother, that he seemed very slight and vulnerable to be taking on such tremendous odds...."

The celebrity is never as we imagine. I saw Robert Redford once at The Sink, a restaurant in Boulder, Colorado. He, too, is a small man, also somewhat below what might be considered average height. He had on jeans and a white shirt, utterly ordinary, despite his stardom and acclaim for directing and producing and starring in all those major movies and television specials and other starry moments. Indeed, that face that we see on celluloid, so large and commanding, was in the low light of the plain Boulder cafe just a small and vulnerable visage, but so familiar. *Don't I know you?*

Didn't we know *you,* Martin?

We did not.

Mostly we used you. Like the last time Martin King visited Denver, on a Thursday—May 18, 1967. An impromptu demonstration by students erupted one block from the University of Denver Arena where he was speaking. According to newspaper accounts, a crowd "numbering about 500 at its peak" was involved. The throng tried to overtake the nearby Valley Highway, but were turned back by police after two crosses were burned and a couple of junked cars stored on a fraternity house parking lot, one bearing a sign "Kill Martin Luther King," were pushed to the scene and set ablaze.

Some students sang "We Shall Overcome" but most were milling about, "restless," according to *The Denver Post,* and the whole incident was treated by the newspapers and by the police as "just one of those little spring annual get-togethers we have," in the words of the police lieutenant helping to coordinate security for the King visit.

Five hundred white students can be excused that way, especially when the incident quickly ended, according to one newspaper account, because "the girl students had to return to their dormitories by midnight."

They had nothing to fear from police and they knew it. And the spring night air was fresh and warm and so were they.

And King's presence on their campus maybe felt dangerous

and exciting, a reason to release their tensions and maybe their anxieties—about being white and blessed while others were dark and, thus, cursed.

King, who had spoken that night against the Vietnam War, and also denounced the U.S. House of Representatives for scuttling a rent subsidy program for poor people, had bravely declared "I love America," adding, "and I want to see our nation stand as a moral example to the world." Earlier, he fielded the usual questions from reporters, including one inquiry about the "prospects of a long hot summer" in America's big cities.

His reply was sober. "A long cold winter" with its lack of creative planning to address the frustrations of Negro citizens was the bigger problem, he answered.

Some of his remarks, heard later by the audience of 2,000, were booed.

In less than one year, he would be dead.

Did we yet know him? We did not. Heroes too quickly become caricatures or symbols. And King, more so perhaps than other contemporary American heroes, has been rendered sanitized and sacred—too pure now for hard analysis or tough debate. Too holy in our memories for the piercing scrutiny that he, ironically, conducted so well on other issues himself. Too much a hero to withstand honest doubt.

So we cringe at the reports of King's weaknesses—the most scandalous, perhaps, the legend of his roving, lonely heart: enjoying "other" women in strange cities, far from his wife and home.

One woman even claims she was with him in the Lorraine Motel in Memphis the night before he was killed. Of course, two of his closest associates, who were at the motel with King the next day when he was murdered, on April 4, 1968, dispute her story. But the denials, and the claims, all fall like so much lead on dull ears when one imagines the small, weary revolutionary out on the road, facing angry crowds and stupid questions— and, after all was said and done, perhaps succumbing to the need to be held close.

Even a visionary is mortal.

Thomas Merton, pondering similar matters, once noted that: "The greatest of tyrannies are . . . based on the postulate that there should never be any sin. . . ."

I'd like to forget the tyranny of "sinlessness"—to hold up my little brown men as holy saints, to follow them blithely along a path of glory to the high ground of forgiveness, love, and total racial understanding.

But the facts of their lives, dug up on my own clumsy search, help me know that high ground is holy ground, but first it's rough ground—and hard to climb. Harder still to stand on.

So King did, indeed, plagiarize portions of his dissertation, acknowledges Stanford University historian Clayborne Carson, hired by the King family to edit his vast collection of papers. King's paper, "A Comparison of the Conceptions of God in the Thinking of Paul Tillich and Henry Nelson Weiman," borrows freely from a 1952 dissertation by Jack Boozer, a theologian who died in 1989, Carson says. Moreover, adds Carson, King borrowed even more from the writings of Tillich, the renowned German-born Protestant theologian whose ideas on "truth" and "being" drove many of the major theological debates of his day.

But curiously, the plagiarism facts—which were "widely rumored and easily available for a year," according to *The New Republic* magazine and other sources—weren't reported at first even by such major newspapers as *The Washington Post*, *The New York Times*, *The Atlanta Journal & Constitution* and *The*

New Republic itself, which later published an 1,800-word article on the "plagiarism cover-up."

A news reporter who wrote the article, Charles Babington, a Washington correspondent for *The News & Observer* in Raleigh who later was hired by *The Washington Post*, explained in his article the media's reticence: "Sentimentality and correct politics inhibited the editors [at *The New Republic*] from vigorously pursuing the story." One editor there agreed. Martin Peretz, editor in chief at *The New Republic*, told Babington, "Everybody suddenly got palsied."

King's halo is just too bright. Nobody wants to dim the light, to take down even by one notch a larger-than-life American icon.

A flawed man? A human being.

As flawed as Gandhi. A man mythologized as a saint—"on a par with Buddha and Jesus Christ," in the words of the last British viceroy of India, Viscount Louis Mountbatten—but a man who nevertheless by his own admission had at least two curious obsessions, both of them seemingly indefensible: the first, his reported refusal to allow doctors to administer penicillin to his dying wife, Kasturbai Gandhi, because injections were "violent." She was suffering from acute bronchitis while sharing jail quarters in Yeravda Prison in Poona with her husband during one of his many imprisonments. Overwhelmed by the bacterial infection, she died in his arms. Gandhi had convinced himself, according to one account, "that the injections would be a violent act, in violation of his belief in non-violence." But the decision seems cruel, a heartless politicized gesture that doesn't square with the Gandhian image.

Neither does Gandhi's admitted curious interests in sexual matters, including his habit late in life of sleeping naked with beautiful naked young women—a practice he defended as a test of his vow of *brachmacharya,* or sexual purity and abstinence.

He had taken the vow at age thirty-six after twenty-three years of marriage and five children. He didn't consult Kasturbai, his wife, whom he'd married when they both were just thirteen—but "make no mistake. I was married, not betrothed," wrote Gandhi in his autobiography, candidly observing, "And oh! that first night."

But, over time, he apparently came to believe that sexual intercourse for pleasure, not procreation, was a sin. After five children, he took his vow of sexual purity, and requested celibacy of his close followers. But finding himself human, he apparently struggled with *brachmacharya*—feeling compelled to test his resolve over and over again.

I encounter an early account of his struggle in his autobiography, *The Story of My Experiments with Truth*, in which Gandhi promises at the outset "not to say how good I am. In judging myself I shall try to be as harsh as truth. . . ."

So I'm not surprised to find more sexual revelations in *Gandhi: A Memoir*, by the late journalist William L. Shirer. He recalls Gandhi giving him a rather curious explanation of *brachmacharya:*

"My meaning of *brachmacharya* is this: 'One . . . who, by constant attendance upon God, has become . . . capable of lying naked with naked women, however beautiful they may be, without being in any manner whatsoever sexually excited.' "

Late in his life, Shirer reported, Gandhi regularly took a woman into his bed at night, including, Shirer says, a grandniece, Manu Gandhi, and a grandnephew's wife, Abha Gandhi. Abha told a Gandhian scholar she was sixteen when Gandhi first asked her to "sleep next to him" during a chilly winter night. After two years, "I began sleeping next to him regularly," she said. But Shirer reported, "As the experiment went on, she said, the old man asked her to take her clothes off."

When the practice became public knowledge, however, a "storm of criticism . . . broke," Shirer said. Gandhi's response to his critics, according to Shirer: "I do hope you will acquit me of having any lustful designs upon women or girls who have been naked with me."

Shirer, who otherwise exalted Gandhi for "his humility, his selflessness . . . his granite integrity," summarized his account of the "naked women" controversy in this way: "Probably we shall never know the whole truth about Gandhi's 'experiments' with lying naked with naked women in the evening of his life, which he regarded as a test for his sexual purity. But on the basis of what has been revealed, one is left wondering whether such experiments were necessary. If Gandhi got the shivers on wintry nights, why not reach for an extra blanket instead of a girl?"

Shirer added, "True, it was a virtue in Gandhi to publicly admit what other men hide. But this strange chapter in the evening of his life is nevertheless confusing and a little chilling to one, at least, who was touched by this man's nobility."

Flawed men. Human beings.

I had sought out the record of their lives, hoping to find their secrets for taking on major foes—nasty adversaries. The Birmingham White Citizens Council and the British crown, among others—those large, institutional giants that feel so powerful, too big for the ordinary person alone to conquer.

Nasty foes—because, in part, they were not just evil, they were duped. So fooled, said Gandhi, speaking in a court of law about the evils of British rule in India, that "[they] honestly believe that they are administering one of the best systems devised in the world . . . ," even though that system effectively froze out the Indian people from the social and economic life of their own nation, leaving them impoverished, mistreated and nearly spiritually defeated.

Of course, elite Indians themselves, operating under the ancient Hindu caste system, maintained their own exclusionary practices, according to which birth dictated the "rightful place"—or occupation—of every Hindu. There were four broad categories: *Brahmans,* the priests and other religious leaders; *Kshatriyas,* the warriors and princes; *Vaisyas,* the landowners, cattle breeders and tradesmen; and *Sudras,* the craftsmen and artisans. Those excluded from Hindu caste society were considered untouchables and restricted to the most menial work— scavenging, street sweeping, latrine cleaning, according to the Shirer book.

But, remarkably, Gandhi himself defended the hereditary occupations, at least, of the castes as "fundamental, natural and essential"—noting in articles in *Young India*, the weekly magazine he founded, that "the law of heredity is an eternal law" that is not based on "inequality." It was orderly, in other words, for every Hindu to have his or her "place," Gandhi argued, noting that "any attempt to alter that law must lead, as it has led before, to utter confusion." He did, however, object to the "untouchable" category outside of the caste system, calling it a "device of Satan and the greatest of all the blots on Hinduism."

He called the untouchables *harijans,* "the children of God," and scandalized orthodox Hindus by bringing into his ashram entire families of untouchables with whom he broke bread and shared work and living space.

But his conservative religious views—on such matters as the sanctity of cows (he believed the ancient Hindu ruling that cows were sacred) and on caste integrity—are well documented.

These facts make me wonder: If even an otherwise coura-

geous, pioneering, progressive and revolutionary leader such as
Gandhi could defend a seemingly evil system as a caste hierarchy that confines people's destinies *for life,* all of us are capable
of wrong thinking and wrong action.

All of us. Certainly me.

I thought, for years, that the proper response to evil policies
was a *polite* response. *Don't make waves.* Even when I was boiling inside, I was smiling—trying stupidly to ignore oppressive
institutional failure, believing that if I was nice enough, maybe
it would correct itself. That was wrong thinking. The result?
Wrong action—or, worse, inaction. Instead, I should have
fought back—placidly, yes, but *actively.* So when I encountered
resistant thinking at Northglenn Junior High School, in the
nearly all white Denver suburb where my parents moved us in
1962, I should've fought back.

The admissions people were surprised to see me, holding my
school records from Denver Public Schools—including my
scores from the California Battery and the Stanford Achievement Test, showing me performing at a tenth-grade level in language and reading when I was in the sixth grade, and at a
ninth-grade level for spelling and an eighth-grade level in "word
meaning" during that same sixth-grade year. My arithmetic reasoning scores were par—I scored 6.9 on math reasoning in the
sixth grade. But the verbal and reading comprehension, for a
sixth-grader, confirmed my potential—my beautiful smiling
teacher thought so, anyway, so she'd marked my straight-A report card with her neat hand, then added a personal note:
"Patricia has done an outstanding job in the sixth grade.... I
know she will continue to uphold her standard of work." My
proud mother saved the documents, carefully folded in small
brown envelopes and signed by that lovely redheaded sixth-

grade teacher lady, Carma V. Richmond, at Columbine Elementary School, Denver.

It was a bright record, as far as most kids' school lives go, and along with the solid A's and B's I'd earned in seventh and eighth grades at Cole Junior High in Denver, made me a reasonable candidate for a successful school life in the suburbs. But a certain coolness settled around me in Northglenn. I found myself ignored by some teachers in classes, although not all. But the cold shoulders weren't just weary—they were sometimes glacial, in one case even hostile. Cold enough it seemed to chill blood— hard and icy and disapproving and maybe just indifferent. That's a hard atmosphere for intellectual vigor, and I slumped. My grades dropped like stones. I earned my first D ever as a student at Northglenn Junior High. It seemed my brain turned to mush in that environment. I couldn't think right, talk right, "appear" right.

One day an English teacher yelled loudly at me, interrupting her lecture, pointing her red fingernail at my face. "Shut up! Cut out that racket right now!" I was dumbfounded. No teacher had ever spoken to me that way. Not this star pupil, this "accelerated" student whose Denver teachers put gold stars by her name, praising her "excellent" work, her good "work habits," her fine ability to "work independently and with others."

Besides, I hadn't made the ruckus in that class. Somebody else had caused the noise, but when the teacher turned to check things out, she saw only me and she blamed only me. Then, after class, she wouldn't listen to my attempts to defend myself. Just ignored me. Just turned her back to me. Just put up that thick wall that looks to dark people like it's impossible to climb over, like it reaches as high as the sky, as far as the moon or even the stars, so it seems there's no good reason to make an effort to scale it, so many just stop trying. I stopped trying at some point at Northglenn Junior High. I sort of gave in and did what was expected of me—which was hardly anything.

My Daddy fussed at me, but halfheartedly. He couldn't figure it out. What's wrong with you? You've never brought home report cards like this before in your life. You'd better buckle down. Start paying attention. Start concentrating.

I tried. Mostly trying to find my place socially. Needing desperately to find friends in this cold world, I spent most of that year smiling, trying to be liked, maybe even loved. But academically, that school year I was sleepwalking. I was dying.

The next year, sophomore year in high school in nearby Thornton, Colorado, I was actually placed in a "slow" English class, among some kids who seemingly could barely read. If this was meant to be an insult, it worked. If it was meant to be a wake-up call, it was that, too. I was embarrassed, hurt, stunned mostly. So I went to the office to request a transfer to the "regular" class, with bright students—bright like me! But the lady at the desk said I couldn't switch without the teacher's approval, and the teacher said I had to "prove" I could do "high" work. Prove I was who I was.

Gandhi would've said I needed to heal my "inner vision"—or *satyagraha,* or a soul force that he defined as "holding onto the truth." *Satyagraha,* by definition then, would have rendered me sweetly loving and coolly confident but so aware what was happening to me that I could've fought what was happening, and overcome!

Indeed, Gandhi made it look so easy.

Those years he was spinning at his spinning wheel, with that smile on his face, that calmness in his bright eyes. And the wheel going round and round, whistling its quiet spinning sound. It was a sight of sheer and utter simplicity. But that lovely sight and that quiet sound would help dismantle no less than the British Empire in India.

I sought out the facts of the story, which can be told briefly, but it is powerful:

In 1668, the East India Company, a private trading firm, was given a lease to the port of Bombay by Charles II. He'd received it as a dowry when he married the Portuguese royal, Catherine of Bragança. The firm was also operating a factory at Madras, where it owned a prime strip of beach property. And in 1690, it secured permission to build a settlement on a muddy flatland that eventually became Calcutta. These arrangements would, over time, lead to the trading company's actually running three-fifths of the subcontinent for its own profit—the only time in modern history when a political state was controlled by a business interest.

When the arrangement unraveled, beset as it was with corruption and appalling mismanagement, Britain's Queen Victoria on Aug. 12, 1858, signed an act transferring the Indian subcontinent from control of the company to the royal crown—and, at the same time, declaring herself empress of India.

India, at that point, was on its knees before the British Empire. And the worst impact, clearly, was economic. One example: The British had flooded India with cheap Lancashire cloth from their country, forcing millions of Indian peasants to abandon their own spinning and weaving—a cottage industry that for centuries had defined and sustained Indian village life, but under British rule had come undone, leaving much of the subcontinent in poverty.

To fight back, Gandhi devised the most simple of strategies. He took up the spinning wheel. He wanted to revive the practice that had once energized Indian village life, while providing work "for the semi-starved, semi-employed women of India."

And for the rest of his life, he spun daily—if at all possible—even spinning while he entertained guests, counseled followers, or addressed public meetings. Setting himself a daily quota of 200 yards of yarn to spin, he then wore exclusively the homespun *khadi dhoti* garments woven from raw cotton fiber spun by his own hands and those of his followers.

Over time, he convinced millions to return to spinning their own cotton fiber. And when his nationalist movement launched a boycott of British products in India, most notably of cheap cotton cloth, the effects on the Lancashire economy back in England were devastating. "Thousands of looms, millions of spindles and hundreds of thousands of workers," according to the journalist Shirer, were idled by the boycott.

In an interesting twist, Gandhi personally visited the Lancashire cotton-mill region during an historic 1931 visit to England. He was warned that angry crowds there might attack him. Crowds did mob him, but they cheered him—mill workers welcoming him as a leader whose struggle to help the poor in India implied a similar empathy for their own "terrible poverty," as Gandhi described their living and working conditions, right there in England.

Then there was the salt.

Earlier, in India, British imperialists passed a hated law—the Salt Act—that approved a government monopoly on the manufacture of salt, imposed a tax on its sale, and outlawed the right of Indians to make salt themselves, something they'd been doing freely for centuries before British rule.

Gandhi, again, quietly struck back. In March of 1930, he organized a small protest march to the sea, a 200-mile trek—lasting twenty-four days—ending at a small town called Dandi near Jalalpur, at the entrance to the Gulf of Cambay. There,

Gandhi planned openly to collect a few grains of salt, in direct violation of British rule.

A small band of fewer than one hundred followers started the march with Gandhi, ignoring ridicule and indifference from British officials who thought the "stunt" was meaningless and bizarre and, thus, would ruin Gandhi's reputation among the Indian masses.

But as a pure expression of civil disobedience, the simple march soon captivated the imaginations and spirits of poor Indian peasants along the route, not to mention the world press corps—which by the dozens was now following the Salt March. Shirer, in his memoir, reported that as the little band wound its way through the Indian countryside, heading toward the sea at Dandi, peasants poured out of their villages to honor Gandhi, throwing flower petals on the marchers and sprinkling water on the roads to keep down the dust in the stifling heat.

Gandhi was sixty-one and undaunted. "We are marching in the name of God!" he told the peasants at his nightly stops. He said evening prayers, then explained his tactics to undermine the hated salt law. At every stop, hundreds joined the procession, and by the final day several thousand were accompanying Gandhi as he went down to the sea at Dandi. There he bathed and purified himself, according to Hindu tradition, then knelt in the sea to collect some salt—an act that, overnight, would ignite the Indian subcontinent in protest against its British rulers.

Martin Luther King, studying this example years later, would recognize the power of withholding cooperation from a corrupt system. But, like Gandhi, he would believe that hate for the men who ran the system was an improper response.

Gandhi, in his autobiography, put it this way: "It is quite proper to resist and attack a system, but to resist and attack its author is tantamount to resisting and attacking oneself." Indeed, if economic liberation was a central theme of each man's campaign of civil disobedience—and it was—spiritual bondage in the form of hate was too big a sacrifice to pay for that freedom.

Thus, *love* my enemy. Why?

Because we are our brothers' keepers.

King in his time tried to tell us these things.

Love your enemies. Because you and they are bound in that network of mutuality that he wrote about from Birmingham jail. *Whatever affects one directly, affects all indirectly.*

Love my enemies. Because I don't have the luxury not to love them. Joseph Campbell, the seer and scholar of mythology, summed it up perhaps best, so I wrote down his classically profound words:

"Love thine enemies because they are the instruments of your destiny."

At Northglenn Junior High, I could've met my destiny. Staged a sit-in. Or mounted a one-person demonstration. This was the sixties, and the spirit would have been ripe for such an unlikely protest. Moreover, this protest would have been simple and quiet, and thus effective in a Gandhian way. No shouting or cursing or fuming. Just quiet, stepping, singing, marching. Simple and lovely, but making a point: Some of the educators there needed a change of heart. The wrong thinking overlooked and even tolerated there, even from a few, was unjust and unjustified. And this, being an evil thing, would have to be resisted. Some school attitudes, not the people perpetuating them, would have to be called out and questioned. And like King and Gandhi and so many thousands of other warriors before me, I could have done this thing sweetly, elegantly, and beautifully. At the same time, I could've shown genuine appreciation to the people there who were kind and helpful and good, and there were, in fact, many such saints there who deserved my thanks and my respect. And God, being good, would've seized the moment for me and created *something* out of it. An eye-opening awareness among those few school people in Northglenn who were narrow that something in their thinking was wrong. And, for me, as well, a new understanding that I was somebody, and should act like it—not rise only to the level of poor expectations. Not react and overreact to white provocation, good or bad. Not be a puppet, but be my whole self. That is indeed a new understanding. A knowing—that the old way was a wrong way, for all of us. And a change would have to come. Inevitably, as it came to Birmingham and to New Delhi, as it came to Montgomery and to the salt beaches at Jalalpur.

To teach and know these things could have been my destiny, but I couldn't see clearly enough then to seize my fate. But God, being good indeed, operates within second chances.

So here I sit now, looking back on these things, and understanding a singular Gandhian principle: Evil in a system must *always* be resisted, by whoever is called for the battle, and in their own way, as long as it's God's way.

God, indeed, will help discern what's truly evil, or what's just human error and should be overlooked. But if a battle is on, He will signal, reminding that it *must* be waged nonviolently but actively—without bitterness and strife and hate for the adversary. But remarkably with love for the adversary, understanding that in racial matters opponents to equality and justice are operating, as Gandhi would say, outside of the truth, and with flawed vision. They *need* love to get healed.

That softness in love, indeed, makes it look weak and passive. But a loving and nonviolent battle—*ahimsa,* as Gandhi termed it—is anything but soft. King, writing in his book on the

Montgomery boycott, *Stride Toward Freedom*, agreed, urging his followers both to love and to resist evil, actively.

And hate isn't part of the picture. Hate is counterproductive. Debilitating and degrading. Hate leads to *more* hate, said King. Then in a truly remarkable statement for 1958, he told the Negroes watching for his signs that they must, therefore, *love* white people, because they need it.

He wrote such things and preached them to poor black, burdened, ravaged people—and the people didn't faint. The people said amen.

Start with love. Let me love *you* so you can love *me*. We are both broken and only by coming together do we close our human circle.

Only flawed men, it turns out, would know such things.

And only a flawed human could believe them.

There was hope for me.

I couldn't fully see how I could grow to love all white people. White people! But there was a hole in my heart from not loving them, from hating them so long, so very much. Or a hole, perhaps, from hating myself for so long, so very much—for despising myself for not being "right."

But King would say, I believe, such hates are interrelated—superimposed on one another, so that as long as I hate others, I can't love myself. And, at the same time, as long as I hate myself, I can't love others.

Gandhi, attempting to resolve this seemingly impossible dual tension, would call on that concept of *ahimsa,* that nonviolent impulse—defined by him as a belief in the universal oneness of all created beings—in response to a clearly exploitative and hateful British rule in India. King did the same thing in the deep American South.

Along the way, there was fasting. And marches. Singing and praying and fasting some more. There was forgiveness.

To defeat an enemy, one must first forgive his human faults. Then attack him, with love. Loving him long enough to change him, to heal him, to awaken him and, finally, long enough to forgive him, then forgive yourself.

The devil, Satan himself, cannot resist this brightness. It is too overpowering. It unleashes a force that won't be contained. Light excelleth darkness, saith the preacher—that Ecclesiastical seer.

And love? It never fails.

Is this my bliss?

I feel curiously light-headed, starting as I am to forgive myself for not knowing in Northglenn what I should've been or done—and starting to forgive those white people there who were fearful and narrow in ways that too often define race relations in the world.

So, Father, forgive us. We were shaped by our past and we clung to it, not knowing we could enact change and still survive each other. I surely survived, despite my ignorance. And now here I sit, writing about love—no longer bothered by that worry that love lets the "bad guys" off the hook. In fact, we were all bad—bad with misunderstanding and hate and resentment.

King, in his beautiful meekness, and in his amazing boldness, fully knew the only way to fix such dislocation, and so did Gandhi. So, said the Mahatma warrior, start "with love and truth."

This may be the colored man's burden. Colored people may collectively have this assignment: to know enough about breakage to start the mending.

A little brown man, *of course,* wrote the rules of love for this century. He was riding on a train when it started. Gandhi, who had traveled in dignity throughout England—who'd enjoyed the privilege of his caste in his native India—one day met his destiny in South Africa, on a train. The metaphor is too large. But suffice it to say that when he got off that train, he would never be the same. Nor would his country. Nor mine. Nor, it turns out, will I.

I'm challenged by Gandhian principles to understand—indeed, to know—that the proper response to institutional injustice is action. But it must be wrapped in love. Therein is the power. And the difficulty. Loving one's enemy is to bury deep one's egoistic tendencies. It requires "a supraconsciousness," the Trappist monk and Gandhian scholar Thomas Merton said, advocating: ". . . the strength of heart which is capable of liberating the oppressed and the oppressor together. . . . In any event, without that capacity for pity, neither of them will be able to recognize the truth of their situation: a common relationship in a common complex of sin."

This coming together—this reconciliation, which often seems so impossible to achieve in racial matters but which must never be given up as an impossibility—can often start, indeed, one by one—giving the other person the benefit of the doubt, assuming somebody just misspoke or misunderstood or made a mistake. And assuming, also, that the other person's inner vision is distorted. And that the distortion doesn't make the other person evil, it just means he or she is human—caught, as Merton says, in that "common complex of sin" and looking, as we all are, for a way out.

Indeed, King spoke of white people *thanking him* for forcing them to change. On the first day of integrated bus riding in Montgomery, Alabama, after the long and acrimonious struggle for this civil dignity, some of the whites even met him with friendly smiles.

But these aren't simple happy endings.

Forgiveness and love assuredly work, but sometimes *slowly.*

In the meantime, there is that inner peace—that peace that passes understanding, and it's curative. That's the bonus, and I have craved it, believing in my soul that anger, as an everyday state, was killing me. Tricking me. Trapping me whole and fast. Any tactic I could apply seemed worthy of serious consideration.

I think, indeed, of Gandhi and his third vow, *aparigraha.* This nonpossession of material things, he said, helped his efforts at discerning truth. When he was assassinated, on January 30, 1948, he owned only a few items—including one pair of spectacles, one pair of worn sandals, one writing pen, and, of course, his spinning wheel.

Owning too many things, he said, corrupted the soul—weighing down a person's ability to reach that truth which he so zealously sought.

In the West, the principle of *aparigraha* seems even more extreme than nonviolence or even, perhaps, sexual celibacy. But I ponder it, for the sake of instruction. And it seems that if I worry less about acquiring the trappings of Western success, I can free my mind to find itself—and my heart fo find my destiny. Because all my life, it seems, I've wanted the things that white people had—swimming pools and sports cars and fancy clothes; wanted them, not for what they were, but because white people had them. Their ownership gave currency to the beautiful things, and my struggle to acquire some of them has taken much time and effort and too many years.

I admire Gandhi's rejection of this ethic of greed, because within it lies an intriguing instinct that is liberating. Racially so.

I'm rather delighted, indeed, to learn that when King left Montgomery in 1959 to move back to Atlanta, he was still driving his old '54 Pontiac. He and Coretta, according to the historian Taylor Branch, who told the King story so well, weren't looking for houses in Atlanta's upscale Negro neighborhoods. He was content to live near poor folks, even after dining and debating with princes and potentates.

I close my eyes, imagining him in the dented, dusty car. He is smiling, with that youthful brightness that Baldwin described so lovingly, humming with the radio tuned to his beloved classical music, perhaps to one of his favorite operas—Donizetti's *Lucia di Lammermoor* or Puccini's *La Bohème* or Verdi'a *Aïda*.

The window is down, maybe blowing his pretty Coretta's hair softly. And they are happy. They are together. They are not bitter.

I like this picture. I like its moral:

Live spare. Be happy. *Then* you can love your enemies.

Love them as Jesus loved the lepers and the thief on the cross and the street-walking woman at the well. Love them as Gandhi loved the silly British royalists, even as he battled to overcome them.

Love them as Brother King loved the Birmingham merchants who blocked his way and the Montgomery ministers who wanted him to wait, but he had to answer them, lovingly, and explain why he couldn't wait another day, another hour.

I study their lessons in love, finding in them a bright, high morality that beckons, shining down on my yearning efforts to get free.

So, now, to them—those meek and mighty warriors—I offer this prayer of thanksgiving:

Thank you, Jesus.

Little brown man, teaching the people and absolving the sinful.

And thank you, Gandhi. Little brown man with your white cotton *khadi dhoti,* spinning and spinning at your loom, reciting your Gujarati stanza—those words, which you said, "gripped my mind and heart." Its precept, you declared, "became my guiding principle:

> "*. . . But the truly noble know all men as one,*
> *And return with gladness good for evil done.*"

Good for evil. King preached that message. And the people didn't faint. Poor black folks—trapped in the misery of their birth—listened to their Gandhi disciple tell them to love white people. Then they shouted amen.

They loved their King. Little brown man in your white shirts and preacher suits. Driving your '54 Pontiac back to Atlanta. Teaching the people. Touching the masses. Starting the love.

Thank you, Martin. Thank you for knowing Gandhi. Then thank you for knowing yourself. Thank you, indeed, masters, for being flawed like me, like all of us—but still, nevertheless, seeking that higher ground. So hard to find, harder still to stand on—that most excellent way. The way of love. The way to life.

You set the mark, and we clearly see you there.

And we hear you.

We are listening.

PART THREE

Love

(Four Stories and

an Ending)

CHAPTER NINE

Real Life

You have a different kind of tenderness for everybody you know.

Allan Gurganus, White People

I am walking on tiptoe, on eggs.

We are arguing in the morning, my husband and I. It's the worst time of day to fight, even worse than the weary, heated blowups that wives and husbands have late in the evening—when they're both tired, when they're not smart enough to fight well, because they're both dumb with fatigue.

But at daybreak, the day is too new to spoil. The covers are still warm. The sky is pink cotton, and the sleeping dog downstairs hasn't yet stretched. It's a time, one might argue, for making love.

But this morning we're lying in bed on our backs, arguing about money.

He wants to spend some. I want to hold onto it with that tightness that makes me believe I am safe. I've been black so long I get nervous over even a little abundance. It might be rigged. Better be watchful. Better be careful. Better apologize if I have some of it. To have even a little money, indeed—that's not authentically black. Proof of that, I guess, is this silly fight. It's still running.

The argument has looped back on itself, and we're sounding plain stupid. "I thought you said that I said that you said you're not gonna second-guess every little penny that goes out of this house . . ."

I can curse when I'm angry, but my husband hates the sound of it. So I am biting my tongue, but a good damn would damn well make the bickering feel damn better.

I kick off the covers and head for the bathroom.

I'm frustrated all around.

And I'm walking on eggs. It's my money we're arguing about—or rather, some extra money that I earned. So that makes it dynamite. The few extra dollars, always so damn precious in a black household, have sabotaged the morning and turned into napalm. And predictably, when we get down to the kitchen—now dressed for work—he ignites it.

"Hey, just forget me, sugar," he says. "It's *your* money. You can do whatever you want with it."

A door slams. He's gone.

But he takes with him the air from the room and he leaves the anger there, boiling. It's old anger. Maybe old as Hannibal. Old like Toussaint and Vesey and Cinque. Bad with its oldness, and dangerous.

He's going off to work—*the man* will meet him there, with all the man's stuff right in his face, at his heart—and I have sent him away vulnerable. Hobbled by anger.

A black woman tries not to do that to her man.

We're supposed to be comrades with our partners. That's what the union can look like, something military in nature. Especially with this man—generous, loving. An ally.

But I'm not a good soldier. I saw fairy tales when I was a girl and I got confused. I thought I could be Cinderella. There would be a prince. And a castle in an enchanted forest, with white horses and velvet dresses and crystal slippers and a stairway brushed bright with gold.

I thought a man would save me.

Why shouldn't I think that?

And ain't I a woman?

With us, from the beginning, there was the color matter.

My husband, Dan, isn't just yellow—but so light-skinned that some days he could be transparent. Deep in the winter, when the sun keeps low and he mostly stays indoors, he is flatly white. There's no way around it. He's "black" officially, of course—according to the U.S. Census Bureau—but his skin is white. Dead pale.

The background of that situation weaves, like the backgrounds of most African Americans, deep across the color line. Truly, we are a hybrid people.

In Dan' family, the drifter was Irish. Last name Daniels. He dallied with Dan's great-grandmother when she was young and lovely. Then he left, as the white men usually did, only verifying his presence with a baby, a son—Dan's pretty grandfather, Jesse.

Jesse was beautiful truly—a squarish, muscular bantam with brown curls and tan skin. He had big hands and a cleft in his chin and devil-green eyes. As he grew, he easily attracted heat and notice because of his good looks. Women craved him. But he hated the drifter who'd left him a bastard, and refused to use the man's last name: Daniels.

Instead, he crafted up an appellation for himself, using, we think, the names of friends or loved ones or benefactors. Somebody's Uncle Ray? An Aunt Bonnie? Nobody knows. But in the end, his name would be Raybon. Jesse Daniel Raybon.

He gave his name to his only son. Then Jesse II gave the name to *his* only son, Jesse Daniel Raybon III.

I married that man.

That's how these things start.

I saw Dan, literally, across a crowded room.

Friday night. A party.

A black studies professor in Boulder was hosting the little reception at his house for a black administrator new to the university. I was new at CU myself, recently enrolled in the graduate school. But when a new acquaintance asked me to drive to the party with her, I stalled a bit. Then I wavered. Then she talked me into going along.

Friday night.

Dan was mingling in the crowd now packed in the professor's basement rec room. I wasn't there five minutes when he asked me to dance. Then he wouldn't go away. All evening, every few minutes, there he was—standing at my side, talking. Joking. Moving in for the slow songs, beating out any other people trying to score. There was a bit of that going on that night. Men pushing their heat and their interest at women. Talking their intellectual games—this was a university after all—but, in the end, simply trying to connect.

Colorado is an outpost and isolation can kill.

So I had to look at this man, try to figure out what he wanted. He had on dark slacks and a dark green turtleneck sweater. His Afro was big, but forced; his hair wasn't kinky. So he'd tried to fluff it into something notable. I thought that was kind of nice. He was trying, with his hair at least, to look sort of black. He was nice looking, but not pretty. So I could talk to him without staring at him. *That* was nice.

But still there was that drifter's legacy, right there. His light skin, if not a wall, was a long fence. I stood back and looked at myself trying to decide if I wanted to get over it.

I had never trusted myself to love light skin on a black man. My model for maleness is my father, that mahogany warrior, and this pale suitor looked curious. I didn't know what he wanted, or why.

But he kept talking and pushing and *being around.*

Next day, the doorbell rang at my apartment. I opened the door and Dan was standing there. He had on jeans and a windbreaker and sneakers. He was talking through the screen.

Some people are playing touch football. C'mon.

I was twenty-five, already divorced, with a four-year-old daughter. Old and young. Black women bring our baggage with us. I'd had my college marriage early on. I'd ended it. Now Lord, I prayed just a week before meeting Dan, send me a man who will help me out. I don't need a boyfriend, I need a mate. A "helpmeet," to use the Bible word. Then I'd forgotten the prayer and gone on.

Be careful what you pray for. You might get it.

Help from a man, saith the Psalms of David, is a vain thing. Dan didn't know this.

If two flakes of snow fell, he came by my apartment to clean off my car's windshield. Then he stole away like a phantom, never asking later if I noticed.

When I ate some bad chicken and threw up, after a movie, all over somebody's sidewalk, he washed it off. Back home, he wet a washcloth with cold water and held it to my face.

He checked the tires on my car and said the pressure was all wrong, then he fixed them. Then he washed the whitewalls with a toothbrush and waxed the finish with one of his old T-shirts.

I didn't know how to process the kindness.

But I was charmed by it. Must be devil magic. This black man with white skin was a conjurer. He could smile at ladies and they melted. Black and brown ladies all giggly at his jokes and his attention, transparent in their enjoyment of him. Maybe it wasn't his color, but maybe it was that luminescence. Blinding luster.

Six weeks after we met, when he told my parents he wanted to marry me, my mother put her hands on her hips and said, *Well*. Then she hugged him. My father shook his hand, then Daddy went to the kitchen to get the good glasses and a bottle.

There was a lot of laughing, along with a complete and utter trust in my right to be a bride. There would be flowers and a white cake and a beautiful church. In my girlhood dreams, this is what love looked like. So, of course, I was terrified.

This man had so much currency in my culture—just because of how he looked. I tried consciously to devalue that part of him, and reckon with him on any other level—his intellect, his character, his sense of humor. And slowly I neutralized his color, willing myself not to see it.

A brown girl has to protect herself.

The day of the wedding, December 20—ten weeks after we'd met—Dan sneaked into the hallway at the church where I was waiting with my sister, my matron of honor.

Dan kissed me and gave me a flower, then showed me how he'd fixed a broken button on his rented tuxedo with a piece of Scotch tape. We laughed. We kissed.

My nervous father shooed him away. "That's bad luck,"

Daddy said. "Seeing the bride before the ceremony, I think that's bad luck."

As payback, perhaps, our first year was a disaster.

The problem was we didn't know each other. Ten weeks is a short, hot courtship. But it's not enough time to reconcile the quirks.

Our differences—his high energy, my low-key pace; his outgoing *out there* nature, my introversion; his spontaneity, my deliberateness—started small, then intensified. We argued. We made up. Argued some more. Made up again.

He would say now that I exaggerate—that we had first-year jitters and we got over it.

He doesn't yet know the struggle I had to find a way to love him: all of him. I'd partitioned him up, leaving out his color. I believed he couldn't know pain—in the way that all black and brown people know it. He had grown up under grace, I believed, because he was "light."

And, indeed, people gravitated to him as if dazzled. I had to *work* to be liked, to get approval. (I saw it that way.) He just walked in a door and faces lit up.

Old resentments and jealousy had their way.

I was envious of my husband's *ease* in the world, as I saw it. But I couldn't explain it because I couldn't see it myself. I just knew that he could laugh quicker and deeper, trust better and sooner, and reach farther. He could even say I love you anytime, all the time. But the words were trapped in my feet.

I'd walked up to the fence but I hadn't crossed it. I'd just gotten real, real close. Lust and sex, affection and deep respect—all these things I shared with him.

But love? I couldn't say it. Not without effort.

So he would ask me.

Do you love me? He wanted to hear it.

Truly, everbody does. *Just say that word.* Do you love me, baby, really *love* me?

Um-mm, I'd say, nodding yes. Thinking, what is love?

Love is an itching in my heart.

Love is a serious business.

So we had a baby.

Five years went by first.

Courage takes time.

She would be pretty and brown like her sister. I could see her already, caramel skin and jet black hair and coal-black eyes. I took my vitamins and stopped cooking with salt. Halfway along, battling the flu, I endured without pills or potions or mentholatums. I wouldn't risk it.

This pregnancy would be natural. And so was my labor, but not on purpose. We rolled into a Denver hospital at 2:00 A.M. on a sleety night in April. At 2:06 A.M., the little brown baby was born, draped in my blood and her mucus, with nurses shouting at us, alarmed at her quick arrival. Then they calmed down and cleaned her and wrapped her in a towel and handed me my little brown baby girl.

She was white.

Light as her father. Lighter, actually, never warmed by the sun. She opened her eyes. *Blue.* Like sky at midday. Like noon in Dublin. An Irish blue, as properly recessive as all the secrets that African Americans carry each in our weary genes. Too much blue to carry, it's so heavy. Oceans of blue, wider than a middle passage, so much of it that I just squinted.

Her gaze was intense, a laser.

I *will* see you. I will take in your face. Just drink it in.

Blue eyes never looked at me like that before. I put my index finger in her right hand. She grabbed it, clinging.

A little white baby with blue eyes, looking and clinging, waiting for my teat.

She needed me.

She hiccuped.

I asked for a towel to wash my hands before I held her close. She was porcelain and clinging to my finger.

I opened her wrapping to look at her. She didn't cry. She let me study her tiny feet and arms and toes. Her skin was warm and white and utterly new.

She looked like everything I had learned so long ago to fear. She was that racial presumption—*light is good; dark is bad*—that had shaped all my early days. And here that knowledge now was lying, sleeping, in my arms. Smelling like sun or clouds or something so clean I couldn't even name it.

I was enchanted, but then I felt fear.

My child was breathing softly, letting me hold her close, but she couldn't guess that even then I was pondering how to love her right—how, with brown skin, to fully be her mother. I could pretend that her color didn't matter, or maybe even pretend it wasn't there.

But an infant is a whole. This little baby didn't come in pieces. I would have to love all of her, or none. And she needed a mother. Jesus, I was all she had.

The next day when she scratched her face with one of her fingernails, and bled, I cried.

I cried for the next two weeks anyway. She needed me. And so did my husband and my baby's older sister—my pretty brown child, now age nine.

My older girl, indeed, was standing warily by, knowing that something new had entered her life but not exactly sure what to make of this tiny infant stranger. I watched her watching the baby, but at first from afar, taking many long days to warm up to this child we called her new sister. As the youngest-born sibling myself, I couldn't imagine how my older child felt now about our household, standing on the sidelines, watching all the fuss about a swaddled little baby. Months later, my big girl told me she was mostly surprised. She'd expected that the new baby would *look* just like her. Yes, I responded. I did, too! But sometimes, I told her, you get a sweet surprise. You have to be ready.

All of them, indeed, were reaching for me now—my husband included—but the baby especially. But maybe I wasn't ready. Maybe I wasn't even worthy, for any of them, but in particular for this baby.

For a lifetime, I'd rolled my eyes at light-skin girls, believing that the look they wore behind their placid faces was assurance and God's mercy and a special magic, all mixed up together. Now I knew something else about that look: It was longing.

So I sang songs to her, then I told her what she needed to hear and what I needed to say. I love you. It was the only way to describe how I felt.

I'd known that feeling when her sister was born brown like me. *That* was love. No need to question.

This bundle nestled at my neck, breathing her little sounds onto my skin, now drew up the same, deep, indescribable tenderness.

But you have a different kind of tenderness for everybody you know. I read that in a book. I think it's true.

For her sister, the tenderness felt familiar, what a mother would expect to feel for her firstborn child. And the world affirmed it. Strangers stopped me on the street. Look at that pretty black baby. *Pretty* black girl. Pretty *black* girl. They were so magnanimous. So pleased that they noticed she was black and pretty at the same time. And, indeed, I felt blessed. God was in His heaven and the planets were aligned. This was supposed to be.

But for this baby, the tenderness was surprise and panic.

She needed me, and she *wasn't* "black." But—and this did surprise me—her needs were no different. Her pain no different. Her joy no different than the myriad emotional highs or lows that make up the ordinary balance of the rest of us.

She wasn't "black," but she was whole. I couldn't carve away her color and throw it out. I'd birthed the child. All of her was part of me, too. The color part now seemed in fact so oddly random, an arbitrary covering that had absolutely nothing to do with *the who* of her. Other people often reacted to it. Peering at her eyes, noticing when they changed from blue to a hazel green, commenting always on her skin. *She's just so light.* But color was not synonymous with her essence.

Call this a breakthrough. I was learning. From this baby I was finally understanding that our *outside* covering simply cannot matter.

I got protective.

When the side-glances started—as my child grew: the low looks under hooded eyes from all the people suspecting her for her color—I wanted to shield her from life itself. How dare the world not adore her *fully,* as I did?

When some church women suggested in whispers that I "favored" the "light" child—projecting surely their own ancient fears—my shoulders squared and I did not act like Jesus. The "dark" child, indeed, now had a special burden to bear: comparison.

But I had *two* children to raise, both lugging the baggage of color, sharing a mother who was mortal.

I needed answers. But mortals get questions.

Do you love me?

Dan's old question was older than his memories of growing up yellow and misunderstood. I listened to it now for the first time, listened hard.

He told me a story. When he was a boy growing up in Richmond Heights, Missouri, just outside St. Louis, he and his sister played all the time with three children—white children—who lived in a house across the street. A dirt road, Woodmont Lane, separated the white families from the black families on that road. But the children played together anyway. All the time— marbles and jacks and dolls and bicycles.

One day, the white children rang his doorbell. They'd come to tell Dan and his sister that they couldn't play with them anymore. Then they turned awkwardly, laughing, and ran back across the road.

A child remembers. Dan knows the details. He can see the white children sneak glances at each other before they blurt out their news. He can see his mother, in her housedress, easing forward with comfort. She wraps her brown arms around her light children to calm the hurt. Later she will tell Dan that other white children had shunned his little white playmates for being friendly to Negroes.

Those poor white children. They are the losers, his mother explains, soothing. You have the best toys, the best snacks and treats, the swing set. You have a black-and-white TV. And pho- nograph records. And a cocker spaniel dog. And now they will miss that, his mother says.

They will miss that.

The ways of love are no mystery.

In the First Book of Corinthians, the Apostle Paul writes to the church of God at Corinth:

Love is patient, love is kind. It does not envy. It does not boast, it is not proud. It is not rude, it is not self-seeking, it is not easily angered, it keeps no record of wrongs. Love does not delight in evil but rejoices with the truth. It always protects, always trusts, always hopes, always perseveres.

Love never fails.

I know now why. Love surpasses all the things that sundry matters—race or wealth or favor or anything else—may mean to wary people. Love is the only thing everybody needs. It's not a prize or a reward or a ticket. It doesn't come easy to one man, and not the other. Or bless one child but not be needed by another. Love always believes. So everybody longs for it. Anybody can give it. Nobody ever wants to miss it.

Nobody ever should.

Six o'clock.

The man comes home from work.

I'm sorry.

I'm sorry, too.

Let's not argue.

We stop counting the precious little money long enough to measure what we really have, what we must not lose. We take account of what we know to be worth preserving. Then each of us, turning toward the other, says with our eyes the same thing.

Hold me.

The heart can slowly find its way.

CHAPTER TEN

Regarding Mother

But you remember this, now. Your mother raised you.
Maya Angelou, Gather Together in My Name

Sooner or later, the black child turns back to her mother. So I find myself thinking more now about mine, wondering how she did it—kept on going, smiling, trusting—when it would've been so easy to stop and give up.

Even first, when her father died and she was just thirteen— just starting to really need the mysterious gifts that a father gives a daughter: the assurances and all the little lessons—even then, after his hard and lingering dying, she didn't give up.

He was the love of her childhood life—a bronze and hand-some truck driver who died an early death after a truck slipped out of gear and crushed him. He'd driven all day for the Thomas & Howard Wholesale Warehouse where he worked in

Durham, North Carolina. He had parked the truck in its stall, then for some reason walked to the front end to crank up the engine again. The truck lurched wildly—suddenly climbing all over him, doing its bad and merciless work. His injuries were grim, internal and deep and persistent. After the accident, a year or so passed and he healed a bit and surely tried to rally, but he never fully recovered. Then his health turned bad. Then he went down fast and, suddenly, one day he was fully gone. Henry Stephen Burnett, her Daddy, was dead.

My mother, called home from school that day, got the hard news and wanted perhaps to die then herself. She mourned him so deeply—the beautiful man with the laughter in his fine face, who had pennies in his pockets that he'd give his children on Sundays and candy to surprise them and jokes to tell them and whistling songs on his lips. And the fruit!—at Christmas, he'd always buy each of his five children one fat sweet orange, one apple, a fistful of raisins and a sprinkling of Christmas nuts—English walnuts, butternuts, laughingly called "nigger toes" by even the colored people, and almonds—plus one sweet stick each of peppermint candy. The peppermint was used as a straw to suck the juice out of the sweet orange. These were delicacies in the Depression years, something only rich folks ate year-round—orange fruit wrapped in crisp white paper, as if each piece were a jewel, and placed with the other fruit in a decorated box on Christmas morning. One for each child. And the smell! So grandly deep and sweet. Only the best Daddies brought home gifts like this, even if he probably got the stuff at cost at the wholesale place where he worked.

But Henry Burnett's children loved it and it was worth the effort to see the children's merry faces on Christmas morning. They weren't looking for much else, just a toy or two that they'd all share—and each year they always got one new pair of roller skates. A working man couldn't buy bicycles for five children. But they needed the skates—they rode them everywhere: school, errands, downtown shopping. And also he could buy those fine oranges once a year. They tasted like heaven. Such a beautiful Daddy. So handsome and wonderful.

And now he was gone.

It felt like the end of the world, my mother would say. Maybe like God Himself had forsaken her—this fourth child, not as "light" as the others, just dark enough so her mother would tease her, call her "my little black girl." Indeed, the color hierarchy is always so carefully chronicled in a hued family. The two boys and an older sister, Catherine—nicknamed Cat—were always described from birth as "fair," meaning "light." My mother and another sister, Blanche, were the "dark" children. Everybody in the family agreed on this. It's odd to me that old photographs hardly show any difference in the skin tones of the five siblings. But at that time, and in that place, color for colored people was like snow in the Arctic. Every slight variation *meant something*. And most colored people, still, know all the possible names—light-skin, red-bone, paper-sack, caramel, cinnamon, high yellow, near white, blue black, Chinese-looking, Indian-looking, honey-color, lemon-color, ebony black, coal black, skillet blond, tar baby, *black* black.

When my mother recites like a script her own family's color distinctions, she is being true to her people, her self, and her time. But when she says those distinctions meant nothing inside her immediate family—that it "didn't bother" her to be called "little black girl" in a house full of light-skinned children—she in the same breath will admit, at nearly eighty, a nagging belief that her mother "always thought much more of Cat," the "lighter" sister.

These doubts linger sometimes for a lifetime.

But my mother knew for a fact that her father didn't, *couldn't,* favor any of his children over the others, and that he loved them all—so clearly he loved *her.* She knows this. His look said so, and his laughter and his kindness, and that charm he spread so easily. His winks and his hugs and even his discipline, which was quick and clear—still, it all felt like full affection.

She reveled in it.

Nothing could diminish it, not even Jim Crow. And not even the family's one spoiler relative, their great Auntie Nannie.

My mother was named for her: Nannie Ruth. It was a name she never liked, and still doesn't, maybe because she still remembers her Auntie Nannie's blatant favoritism—like the time Auntie Nannie sewed beautiful new outfits for my mother's two brothers and light sister, but didn't bother to make outfits for my mother and Blanche, the "dark ones." My mother's Daddy was furious. He called up short this Aunt Nannie, telling her never to come bearing gifts for his children unless she brought gifts for *all* his children.

He was a champion, this Daddy. And he was bronze like my mother and he adored her. Surely loved her as much as the light children, maybe more, but certainly as much. Loved them all. So when he died, she was inconsolable—until a family friend called her aside to tell her that death, like birth and life, just happens. She wasn't special because of this death—not persecuted more or harmed more than anybody else who'd ever lost a loved one. And she'd have to get over it.

So my Mama, who is not anything if not uncomplicated, listened to this advice and decided, yes, OK.

She got on with it over time, that being her life in North Carolina tobacco country, where "the college"—North Carolina State College for Negroes—employed seemingly half the black folks in her hometown, Durham, and the North Carolina Mutual Life Insurance Company, founded and owned by Negro entrepreneurs, employed the other half. And everybody was expected to buy an insurance policy and go to the college at some point and get a degree.

It was a good life, even with the South's stupidity.

"We just had so much *fun,*" my mother says.

Five children in one house can make good mischief—like the summer nights they'd tie a string to a length of rubber hose, lay it in the grass alongside the front of their house, then—when some unknowing person came walking along—pull the fat black hose slowly across the sidewalk. Snake! Women would throw up their purses and men would high step into the night, whooping with alarm. And the five Burnett children would holler with their laughter, lifting their voices into the starry Southern sky.

Or there was the time her oldest brother, Frank—nicknamed Brother—decided to raise chickens in their backyard. "One day the doorbell rang," my mother says, "and here comes this mail-order delivery man with box after box for Brother—long flat boxes with little holes in the top—and inside were all these chickens. Not ten or twenty—*one hundred* chickens."

Her brother turned the chicks loose in a homemade henhouse, not figuring that the little birds would be small enough to crawl through the cheap chicken wire. So chickens were everywhere and Brother, the ever popular and busy boy, always seemed to be down the block at the colored tennis courts or playing with friends, never at home when the chickens got loose. "My other brother, Henry, and I would have to run out there and try to shoo them in the henhouse—like when it started to rain," my mother recalls. "But every step you took, you'd stomp on one. And intestines would just go flying! It was the biggest mess. All those fuzzy yellow biddies running around, and guts squirting out. And the noise!"

She gets quiet for a moment, then starts chuckling. It's her high, long laughter—so familiar to anybody who knows her—and it's a contagious laugh, so I start to chuckle, too. "It really was funny," she says. "It was just a mess. But Henry and I would just be laughing, calling for *Brother!* And those poor chickens. I don't think a single one of them lived to be three months old. But it was just another one of our adventures."

She is smiling.

Hers was a family that knew how to laugh, that understood fun.

So the fun stories got saved, and so did the memories. And, combined, they make up a testament about surviving at a time when colored people could've easily just dropped and died from their bitterness. The South and their America was that bad.

But in my mother's home, her Daddy set his own new tone, pulling up in the wholesale company's truck at their house on Fayetteville Street, honking the horn loud, calling for all the children to climb in the back while he made his local deliveries. He had a brightness, this man—and optimism and a steady cheerfulness that, despite his strictness, permitted fun.

Indeed, he personified a pivotal truth—that if you're fully loved inside your family, it matters less what the people *outside* that bosom think of you. Even white people couldn't dim this light, not enough to damage you. Love, when it's that broad and confident, can survive even Jim Crow.

My mother, blessed by God with such a family and father, would grow up to understand this truth, even in the South, even if she never would explain it that way, in such words. But she will tell you how her Daddy drove up in that truck, and all the children piled in happy—knowing for sure they'd have some fun that day. Riding along, they'd sneak open a box or two of store candy—Baby Ruths or Hershey's chocolate—then they'd eat their fill, then quick they'd wipe the chocolate off their dusty faces and hands, trying to look innocent.

"Daddy must have known," my mother says, recalling these times, "but he never got after us." And her mother never stopped the fun, never fretted that riding in the back of an open truck with heavy boxes piled around them, rattling down dusty Durham streets, was unsafe. So they were always so glad for these unexpected trips, so happy to see their steady Daddy, blissfully pleased to crawl in his big Thomas & Howard Company truck and take a fun ride around the North Carolina countryside.

A famous child psychiatrist, Foster Cline, says that when "the magic people" in a child's life let her know that she's OK—that she's loved and valued—most everything else that happens, even bad things, can be tolerated and sometimes even shrugged off. This is unequivocally true of my mother and her life.

She lived, indeed, in the misdirected South. But fate or the Almighty had placed her in an upstart Southern place, this brash town Durham, inside a functioning family, surrounded by busy, affirming, and productive Negro people. It wasn't perfect—far from it. But it was nicely livable, and livability suits oppressed people. They can start to thrive. W. E. B. Du Bois, visiting Durham in 1912, credited black Durham's vigor to "the disposition of [white] Durham to say 'Hands off—give them a chance—don't interfere.' " The result was a viable Negro economy with steady progress. "Nobody rented on our street," my mother says. "A big family living on the right ran a neighborhood store next to their house. They had a big backyard and always had wagons, horses, and buggies. On the left was a public health nurse, Miss Pearl."

Next to Miss Pearl lived the dentist, Dr. Hunter. Across the street diagonally was a big fancy house owned by the neighborhood physician, Dr. Mills. "He delivered all five of us right there in our house. The Harris family lived next to Dr. Mills. They had twin girls, slightly younger than me, but we always did things together—tennis and swimming and other things."

In Durham, there were enough rich white people—tobacco and cigarette company big shots, and scholars and doctors at Duke University and lawyers who managed their lives—that the city had a small cultural life. This was for the whites, all of them trying to shake off the city's rough tobacco-town image. But a few white city officials even got a library and a swimming pool and a brick high school built on the colored side of town. One of the state's affluent lawyers, a progressive town booster named John Lathrop Morehead, arranged things so my mother got a job as a cashier at the Hillside Pool for Negroes. He knew young Nannie because her mother, Laura, had taken in the Morehead family laundry for years. Then after my mother's Daddy died, her mother went to work "in service" at the Morehead mansion as the family's maid.

My grandmother, Laura, worked for the Morehead family almost until she was seventy, long after her benefactor, J. Lathrop Morehead, was dead and gone. In the end, she and Mrs. Morehead—fondly called Dougie by her husband and friends (her birth name was Caroline Douglas Hill)—would putter around the Moreheads' big house in Durham, trying with failing hearing to listen to each other's old stories, sharing big cups of black coffee or pekoe tea. Mrs. Morehead, a few years younger, died first. My grandmother cried at her funeral.

The lives of American blacks and American whites cross in odd ways. Poor black folks, working for rich white folks, see things—how the other half lives and eats and entertains and gets educated. This family named Morehead over time nearly adopted the widow, Laura, and her five children—"adopted" in the sense that the Moreheads succored them and did them favors, in their segregated little town, and taught them their ways.

This was no small thing.

The Moreheads were well placed in Durham life, indeed in North Carolina. J.L.'s grandfather, John Motley Morehead, was a governor of North Carolina from 1840 to 1844. His father, Eugene Morehead, established Durham's first bank. And J.L., after serving as alderman and city attorney, ran one of the city's most prominent law practices. If there were richer white people in Durham, and there were, the Moreheads still were rich enough.

So when my mother and her brother, Henry, worked at various times at the *Morehead* mansion—Henry doing yard work and chauffeuring, and my mother ironing and cleaning and cooking with their mother to save money for her college tuition—they were all getting a curious education. Firsthand, they saw the style of Southern privilege—with all its pretty, awesome touches—and my mother learned the basics of it: how to carve fowl and make butter molds, iron creases and whiten linen, set a table and polish silver, arrange flowers and lay a buffet, entertain guests and write thank-yous and cut hair ribbon on the bias so it doesn't unravel. My mother, at nearly eighty, can still entertain twenty-five, thirty, even fifty or more people without a hitch at almost a moment's notice—using now her own china, crystal, silver, and table linens in that patrician style perfected by countless black women whose mothers or grandmothers first saw it themselves from the servant's end of a maid's uniform.

My mother doesn't apologize for this knowledge, or her appreciation of it. She would, indeed, defend criticism that the

Moreheads had no reason *not* to be generous with their knowledge, if not with their wealth. At the same time, my mother knows the Morehead family didn't have to extend their many kindnesses, nor did they have to allow that curious familiarity that springs up so often between blacks and whites in the South.

So J. L. Morehead helped my mother get that summer cashier's job at the new colored swimming pool. When my mother graduated from college and applied for a charge card at the downtown Belk's Department Store, Mrs. Morehead helped her get the card approved. (With it, my mother bought her first fur coat—"actually rabbit pelts," she says with a laugh.) And when my mother married my father, on September 3, 1943, in a "pretty" but modest ceremony in my grandmother's living room, both J.L. and Mrs. Morehead came to the wedding, huddling easily in Laura Burnett's front parlor among the flower arrangements and the colored neighbors and friends. My mother hadn't planned to invite them, she says, but Mrs. Morehead politely hinted for an invitation. So my mother called the wife of John Lathrop Morehead, grandson of the former governor of North Carolina, and invited them to her wedding to Lieut. William Amos Smith at 1208 Fayetteville St.

For a wedding gift, Mrs. Morehead gave my mother several starter pieces of sterling silver flatware—which my mother still owns and uses for "company." She later completed the set.

The sterling pattern is called Repoussé.

Didn't you resent the Moreheads, even just a little?

My mother thinks about this, shrugs, then says a certain no. She didn't resent them their wealth, or their position, or the obvious differences in their fates—all of this determined, of course, by birth.

"They were the only white people I really knew when I was

growing up, and they were good people. Very good," my mother says. She is sitting in her comfortable kitchen in suburban Denver, just hours home from a two-week trip to Durham to see relatives. So these things are fresh on her mind. She saw reminders while she was there—Morehead Avenue and the freeway built on land where the Morehead mansion once stood.

She even gets out the sterling, showing me the first pieces in the set—her initials engraved by Mrs. Morehead on the back of each ornate piece. What did such a gift really mean? Was Dougie Morehead patronizing her maid's daughter, gifting her with such extravagance, even having it monogrammed? Or maybe Mrs. Morehead had grown sincerely fond of this bright woman, this Nannie Ruth, whom she'd known since she was just a girl—and could envision for her a life bigger than the one ordained.

For the next few years, Mrs. Morehead on holidays would send my mother a piece of sterling Repoussé. "It's actually kind of a gaudy pattern," admits my mother, sitting in her kitchen, putting one of the heavy spoons back under the felt in its box. "I would've chosen something more plain, more conservative. But Mrs. Morehead had started it, so I kept buying pieces until I finished the set."

Part of me wants her to say these things with sarcasm and bitterness, but there's no hurt there. And her heart is big. She has only good feelings about these white people who, despite their kindness and "goodness," subscribed to Jim Crow rules in Durham as much as anyone.

My mother snaps shut the silverware case, then tells a story that makes her laugh. She's already chuckling.

"One time, mother and I went to see a movie at the Carolina—the only movie house in the city that admitted Negroes to a 'colored' balcony—and we ran into the Moreheads.

We had bought our tickets at the colored entrance on a side street, climbed the stairs—winding steps going around and around, up and up," my mother says, pointing skyward—"and we took our seats."

They weren't really thinking, she says, about the white people seated on the first floor in the plush seats below. "That's just the way things were. I don't remember worrying about it much . . ."

After the movie, "We walked backed down the steps, and came around by the front of the theater, on our way to the Fayetteville Street bus—and here come Mr. and Mrs. Morehead out of the same movie, out from the 'white' entrance."

So happy to see them!

"Hey Nannie Ruth! Hey Laura!"

"So we greeted them just as cheerfully. 'Hey Mr. Morehead! Hey Miz Morehead!' "

Each pair then turned and strolled into the night, back to their proper parts of town, still happy at the surprise of seeing one another, none of them thinking it odd, my mother says, that the rules of that era—with black life and white life so deliberately separated—required them to watch the same picture from different locations in the same theater, then leave from different doors. One close. One far. One high. One low.

College. Too little money.

To pay the tuition, my mother worked every other semester, then took classes—finally graduating in 1940 at age twenty-four from Virginia State College for Negroes with a bachelor's degree in physical education and science.

She still has her college scrapbook, with photographs and clippings and souvenirs—these things saved now for more than fifty years—that suggest a carefree and privileged life, actually not unlike the Moreheads', but of course *nothing like* the Moreheads' life, but patterned after it anyway. So there's a yellowed newspaper clipping from the colored newspaper, the *Carolina Times*:

LOCAL GIRL GOES TO VA. STATE

Miss Nannie Ruth Burnett left Wednesday morning for Va. State College in Petersburg, Va. where she will continue her studies in Physical Education.

Party invitations, embossed with pretty inks, fill one page of the scrapbook, and notes from friends, a crumpled party favor, lots of poetry and photographs and two softly faded lace-paper doilies—pale pink and pale green, souvenirs from my mother's sorority initiation tea on May 8, 1939—fill the other pages. Her pledge sisters signed the book in their delicate scripts, with their earnest words:

"Dear 'Sister' Nannie: May you sail on the ship 'Ambition' and enter the harbor 'Success' in all that you attempt to do. Didn't we have fun working in the pledge club?! Love Betty S. (Hartford, Conn.)"

Other handwritten notes, thank-yous for favors or courtesies or weddings gifts—the nuptials announced with elegance and restraint in colored newspapers—are also carefully pasted to the pages, every note properly personalized and sincere, some of them worthy of Emily Post herself:

Dear Nannie—
This is to thank you for the lovely gift. Pillow cases are always useful, and these are also beautiful.
Thank you so very much . . . Ethel B.

Her school friends often have nicknames—Snooks, Kitten, Biv, Bif, Dot, Kat, Cat, Kit, Dolly, Pep, Smitty, Baby.

They sign their names with happy salutations. Lots of Luck! All the best! Happy days and all success to you!

My mother's snapshots:

Wearing a riding outfit, complete with boots and crop.

Sitting on the dormitory steps with friends.

Archery class, bows drawn. Matching outfits.

Fencing competition, masks on, épées crossed.

Splash Party in (Va.) State's pool.

Posing by the library.

In her own journal, many years later, my mother writes about meeting my father during the "war years," when enlisted black soldiers were posted to Camp Butler, North Carolina, and an air of urgent love and risk was in the air.

My mother's thoughts:

"We had a good time (all single women). Mrs. Martha Merrick would take a busload of us to Camp Butler to a dance each Friday night. We met some nice fellows (but some country, rude nerds). Some of the girls even married. . . . Then the (black) officers came to town! Mother had two officers and their wives staying in our house. On Sundays, one of them would bring other officers to the house to visit. One of these officers was Lieut. William Amos Smith." (He, of course, would become her husband and, six years later, my father.)

"We (all my bunch) had a ball all that summer. The pool director, Coach John McClendon, would let us have swimming parties after the pool closed for the day. Three or four doors down from my house, Mr. and Mrs. F. K. Walkins turned their home (first floor) into an Officers Club. The black officers didn't have any place to go at night. The enlisted men had the U.S.O over in Hayti (another colored part of town). So we would always go down the street to the Officers Club every night or we'd go to the movies.

"On Sunday afternoons, we would all sit on Mother's porch swing and drink our iced tea and watch the folks pass by. You always knew everybody and they would wave and speak, 'Good evening!' . . ."

There is a gentility in these memories that evokes a certain ease—and a sufficiency. I am intrigued that my mother enjoyed a real completeness in her all-black existence—schools, churches, neighborhoods, library, colleges, and social events—that dares to suggest that white people, with the exception of maybe the Moreheads, didn't matter much in her early life. And, indeed, maybe that was a good thing.

In their isolation, Negroes in Durham looked within and found what they needed.

Affluent blacks built their own tennis center in Durham— the Algonquin Tennis Club, not far from my mother's house. Their pretty privileged children would walk down Fayetteville Street in their white tennis shorts and white tops and white tennis sneakers, swinging their expensive rackets, on their way to the club. My mother and her brothers and the other poor children in the neighborhood improvised. They made tennis rackets out of wood, more like paddles. "But some of those kids could really play with those paddles," my mother recalls. "They'd beat the best of them." So the rich black men started organizing tournaments, and black kids from Raleigh and Greensboro and other cities would come over for the competitions. Everybody would crowd the sidelines and watch. "Many years later, I think, Arthur Ashe played there," my mother says.

If there was social pressure in Durham for blacks, it came less from white people than from well-to-do blacks, and Durham had its share of them.

"We called them the muck de muck," confides my mother, who still uses the term for fancy rich folks. "But everybody knew them all and they knew everybody." One of her best friends married into one of the founding families of the North Carolina Mutual Life Insurance Company, which in a recent year, 1994, reported $9.2 billion in active policies and $54.4 million in premium income.

My mother is aware, matter-of-factly, of such information. So she fully understands—because of such facts—that colored people can be whatever they want to be if they know how to dream. It's not just a vague concept to her. She grew up watching such accomplishment among blacks and aspired to emulate, if not the scale of such achievers, at least their style.

And white people?

"You didn't think about them much."

This is a remarkable statement for a woman born of the South, in a state where everything from the beaches to the ball parks was segregated. The soft cushion that was my mother's family protected her from the things that should have killed her—or at least should have made her give up. The harsh reality of race-based discrimination in the South has been documented. It was damaging. But in her family photos, she is smiling.

In her family memories, she is bright.

In her school scrapbooks, she is pressing upward.

Even on a page honoring her dead loved ones—her father, dead at forty-four, but also her two sisters, Catherine, dead of spinal meningitis at twenty-six, and Blanche, suddenly taken ill while teaching at Morrisson Training School for Colored Boys in nearby Hoffman, North Carolina, at twenty-one, as well as friends who, in that era before vaccinations and immunizations, were so vulnerable and often died quickly and young—my mother's handwritten notation, in red ink, spells out her un-shaken belief about these beautiful dead people, all gone too soon from her life:

"Just asleep."

Hope is a curious trait.

In race matters, hope is the tether to God. Hope is a light in the dark corner. It is that steady, quiet music that keeps on play-ing like a song running in the back of the head—with words promising that life can be OK.

Hope is my mother.

That might've been her name. But since it wasn't, she ab-sorbed that aura of hope and shared it, spread it, offered it, promised it. And this gift of hers surely saved her life, but also certainly my own. In the darkest moments, the bleak situations, after bad decisions and hard lessons and doubting hours, she was always there in the background holding up her durability and that will and her faith and simple encouragement that always believed: Things will be all right.

She should've thought otherwise. People she loved had died, quick and fast, all around her. And life's rules were all fixed, working fully against her. And the world was rude. So she re-members, even now, the young white Morehead cousin visiting J. Lathrop's mansion one day, sitting on the garden patio, enjoy-ing the cold Coca-Cola that my mother had just served him on a silver tray. The young man had been talking with Mrs. Morehead about the new hot book, *Gone with the Wind*, and Mrs. Morehead had offered to lend him her copy. But in that same instant, she gestured to my mother. "Nannie Ruth's reading it now. When she's finished, you can have it."

My mother, telling the story today, can still describe how the young man looked up at her, dumbfounded. Then she shows me how he pointed his finger in her direction, asking his silly question: "*She* can *read?*"

Mrs. Morehead quickly defended her. "Nannie Ruth's in *college*. She's going to the Virginia State College for Negroes in Petersburg!"

But these words—*she* can *read?*—recalled now almost sixty years later, still ring their dull stupidity in my mother's lovely graying head and she hasn't forgotten the sound.

She hasn't forgotten the insult of being brown in the hard South. Or her first teaching job, up north in Westchester County, New York, at a fancy school in Mount Kisco for rich white children, where a child of *the* New York Whitney clan, a four-year-old sprite, felt justified in correcting my mother's Southern black diction. "It's *door*, Miss Burnett. Don't say *do'.*"

The child knew her place and held it.

My mother, watching and hearing these things as they happened to her, never got bitter. Miracles are also unexplainable.

So after she married and moved to St. Louis, and later to Denver, my mother encountered the white people there and the little insults that were inevitable in those places, but she managed always to see the gold in *individuals*.

I suppose I always knew this about her, but somehow the information got lost in a household that she didn't dominate. So I watched her being neighborly—offering her mint leaves for tea and arranging her cut flowers in glass jars and sharing them with white neighbors and Mexican American neighbors, with anybody who looked like a friend—but because most of my own interactions with white-looking people were so false, I concluded that her overtures were phony, too.

It's taken me this long to understand that she was being herself. She meets life and people head-on, one-on-one. And her smile and her friendship are genuine. So amazing.

Her dealings with me were surely just as real. There, indeed, is not one fake note anywhere in my mother. What you see is everything you get, so she is very easy to like. Easier, maybe, to love.

If she learned late in life how to *say* I love you—finally, indeed—she says it now eagerly and urgently, knowing that such words, and the knowledge of this emotion, deeply matter.

Certainly, she learned the gestures of love early in her life, from a magic father. Hers looked on her and caught that spark that is born with every child, and he polished it. It was the best thing that ever happened to her, it protected her all her life, and as I grew, every once and a while, she would rise up and glow—in the strict atmosphere in my father's household—and her bright light would remind me that everything—the race matters and the social dilemmas and the life problems—would somehow get worked out and be OK. For years, I couldn't accept this truth. It seemed too simple. But, still, it was conveyed somehow by my mother. So I guess I stored up this understanding for now, when I hungrily need it. In all of that, therefore, my mother kept me afloat.

She did this with her life. She understood, long before me, that racial peace is not just a crazy idea. Or an odd joke. Peace, in any form, is priceless, she would say—maybe, indeed, because life is so terribly short.

There is a lesson there, indeed, for certainly anyone.

Now in a photograph from her childhood, my mother

stands closely among her handsome family—the light children and her sister, Blanche, around her with her mother and Daddy—and she is leaning with her brothers and sisters into the family bosom, all of them there together, standing in front of the house on Fayetteville Street, right there in the American South, confident and smiling.

She looks happy. And Mama looks smart.

She still is.

CHAPTER ELEVEN

School Daze

But first I have to go to the place, move the dirt, find
why I am there.

Toni Morrison

In the end, we shake hands.

They say thank you or good job, or maybe they say nothing,
then they take their leave of the campus and head for life. At
first, I envied my young white students—with that casual air of
entitlement that some of them have, that attitude that understands their right to be here—to be *served*—by the University of
Colorado in lovely, luminous Boulder. And it is beautiful, with
its leafy, airy clarity. The town's flawless snow. Its sunny cold
sky. Its high, clean brightness. So I also envied the white students' their youth, and the promises of youth. New chances and
new hope and all that energy. And the time that youth has, it
seems, to enjoy it all.

But envy doesn't cover it.

In fact, I mistrusted my students at first. I expected, because they are white, most of them, that they would be spoiled and rich and indifferent to learning and also to me. I assumed they had read D'Souza and Kimball and Bloom—and that they believed what they'd read. And I assumed that, because they were white, they wouldn't greet me with goodwill or, blessedly, even with neutrality. But with suspicion and fear.

And how could they not? More than one critic, Dinesh D'Souza among others, had warned them that in higher education the dreaded affirmative action policies ". . . make it more respectable within the university for minority-group members to be admitted or hired without reference to the reactionary notion of academic merit."

Colleges, indeed, have taken up "unusual practices," he'd said: ". . . accepting minority members even when no particular faculty vacancy exists and when the applicant's field of specialty doesn't correspond with departmental needs. . . ."

So of course these students would think the worst of me, wouldn't they? Certainly, when I walked to the blackboard that first day in 1991 and wrote my name, a blond girl suddenly and fully stood up. "I'm in the wrong section," she called out. Then she gathered her book bag and fled the overheated room. Her alarm and her departure, so hasty and urgent, felt like a rejection. But maybe it wasn't. But possibly it was, and I couldn't deny that possibility.

"What's your background?" a student asked when I later invited their questions.

I was writing news stories before some of them were born, so I gamely reviewed my experience. I showed them my writing. Cited my awards, my degrees, my *qualifications*. I endured the ironic indignity of being interrogated by nineteen-year-olds who perhaps all couldn't spell "interrogate" but believed they had the right to question my qualifications to teach them spelling and reporting and writing and grammar.

And I cowered at first. A white onslaught once did that. The act of being questioned by white inquisitors, no matter how young or how unreasonable, left me feeling angry—but also defensive. And guilty, too, of whatever they suspected.

And logic didn't compensate. It's as if their need to ask confirmed the integrity of their suspicions. So in my case the skills that seemed adequate—perhaps even exemplary—when I walked into the classroom after a busy newspaper career suddenly felt paltry when questioned by white examiners.

So I panicked. I had fifteen weeks to teach them, but only minutes it seemed to convince them I could do it. And my anger about my predicament wouldn't solve my predicament. So I did a curious thing. I comforted them.

I told them they were smart and bright, and that I eagerly awaited the fruits of their labor, which was all true, but I could've held back. Instead, I told them they would help me teach them because they knew, more than I, what they'd paid to learn—so I would try to teach what they needed.

I learned their names.

I told them jokes.

We laughed.

I asked their histories. They told me lineages and legacies and legends. Of immigrant pasts and family pressures, of all-white towns and quiet streets and divorced parents.

I looked closer.

They weren't all nineteen. They weren't all rich. Some had shadows under their young, blue eyes and frowns over their weary brown. Some had hair streaked gray. Some talked of long hours at low-paying jobs where mean wages barely covered the rent and the books and the tuition. Some spoke of spouses and sick babies and cheap apartments and meager meals. They talked of money, of wanting to earn it because it seemed to them there was never enough of that long, green madness. So they were hungry. They were tired. And they cried, some of them, in the secret of my little office, about their fears—their guilty doubts, their proscribed views, their weary American hearts.

So in time I confessed my own sins—my fears of failure, my bitter soul, my deep-set anger. My weary American heart.

Our space was crowded, in truth, with all our "stuff"—race and gender and generational distance. And the atmosphere in our academy was thick with lies and whispers about "preferential treatment" for "protected classes," and the coded language of the times was known by all concerned.

But we had to cut through it all. In order to teach my students, I had to look on them in ways I needed for myself. And that surprised and challenged me—that they needed what I needed: affirmation. Indeed, to teach them I had to actually love them, or at least learn to love their potential. How else could I prove that I could teach?

But that pressure felt like a wet weight on my old and nappy head. Because it seemed, I feared, no matter how well or how poorly I did, whatever I did for them would never be enough.

I opened my bag of tricks. Nothing fancy fell out. All I could teach was what I know—news story "structure" and fact-gathering and interviewing. Very plain stuff. It is so ordinary, so unremarkable—my curriculum. But I know it's so crucial for our times, for our democracy. But it didn't feel *academic*. If I was an imposter, as D'Souza and many others suggested about minority faculty, it would show up in my topic. And my topic was ordinary—newspaper journalism. And my credentials, at the most my master's degree, didn't match up with the academy's best: the doctorate. These were sure measures, and I'd come up short.

And people were watching, then weighing.

So I picked up an already merciless pace and I poured on the work. Piles of work. Tons of work. I worked those lovely white children so hard that first semester—fearful of not being enough for them, of living down to the critics' low expectations of dark people like me—that I fairly killed them and myself as well. It was obscene. What I asked of them and of myself was inhuman and unfair. The pressure to be black and immortal and acceptable drove our agenda like a mania. And the students didn't deserve it. Neither did I.

When the semester ended, my teaching evaluations for that course, Public Affairs Reporting, were solid—an average A rating from the students. But the course itself was rated a B, in part because of the workload, and students complained on their evaluation forms. "Too much work!" "Tried to cram too much material into course." "This should be at least a five-credit class!" "Work load is tough, especially for only three hours of credit." Or, as one student summarized, "We do have lives and other classes outside of the School of Journalism!"

My news editing course also got a B rating, and so did my teaching in that course, but I actually expected a lower rating—and maybe deserved it. I was less confident with the subject matter and the students detected my discomfort. So some challenged me, and I floundered.

One day when I stood at the blackboard to talk about column widths and pica measurements, my mind went blank. My brain wouldn't connect with my mouth. I mumbled some sort of excuse, then finally, with a line of sweat forming on my forehead, announced we would cover the subject the next class session.

The students shifted in their seats, looking embarrassed. Their black professor was not perfect. In fact, I didn't then feel like a professor, and most days still don't. The title "professor" implies a certain level of accomplishment that none of us probably really know how to measure. Professor? That means savior and seer and sage. All I do is *try* to teach.

It should be a simple thing—this teaching, this sharing of skill and insight with willing and hopeful students. But of course it isn't simple. Teaching is a hard thing—like breaking rocks or hoisting bricks. And the hard parts have to do with the work itself and also with the nervous nature of "the academy"—but also with the nature of our times. Which are changing. So some people are teaching Zora Neale Hurston and some are teaching Georg Wilhelm Hegel—and some of us are caught in the middle, not quite sure how we got to be smart or so evil, depending on who is holding the scales.

Doubts nagged me every day that first year, in fact. But I was surprised to learn that doubt seems to permeate all the faculty ranks, top to bottom. It's a clinging self-questioning, characteristic perhaps of people assigned the task of conveying knowledge.

"Let me tell you something," a tenured white male told me one day, after listening to my litany of doubts. "We are *older* than our students. On that basis alone, we know more than they do." He laughed, but there was pain in his eyes. I winced. Then I threw myself headlong into teaching.

That first semester, indeed, teaching consumed half my week; preparing to teach consumed the other half. But I also commuted ninety-eight miles every day, from Denver to Boulder and back. I drove my daughter's after-school car pool, an additional twenty-six miles three days a week. I wrote—and I published. I gave talks. I attended seminars. I held office hours. I loved my husband. I longed for a friend.

I graded papers. I bolted fast food. I neglected my house, my car, my dog, my health. I got sick and a lingering "stomach" ailment was finally diagnosed—a ruptured ovarian cyst, uterine fibroids, and a tangle of abdominal adhesions that had fused a section of my uterus to a portion of my intestines. Over Christmas break I had a hysterectomy. Six weeks later, I returned and took up my full load, sore and in pain. I had shed blood for this job and, in the course of that, given at least one of my reporting students "the best instruction I've ever had at CU," as she wrote inside a holiday Christmas card. I'd also, however, disappointed some, including one who "wished this instructor knew the subject she's supposed to teach."

But, assuredly, I opened the rest of my mail. One was a postcard, neatly typed, so it looked friendly. But this is America and race still matters.

"I assume, like Anita Hill, you are a product of 'race-norming' exams and other tender boosts by a kowtowing government bent on lifting you through college and onto the staff of a state university.... I wonder how many white males with better credentials were shunted aside by the U of C to make way for you?"

On American TV, all white people are beautiful and have good teeth and are smart. In real life, white people have split ends and pimples and ordinary lives and bad grammar. And some are even afraid.

They are like me.

"I don't know what I'm doing in this program," a student, a young woman in glasses, is saying. She has grabbed a Kleenex from the big box on my desk. She is dabbing at her eyes. She doesn't think she is good enough for newspapering. Actually, on this day it seems she doesn't think she is good enough for anything. She wants comfort and advice. I dispense assurance, or try to.

She has come to me, I believe, because she has discerned that I might be willing to listen. I try anyway to listen, I suppose, because I know what it's like not to be heard, or seen. So I'll also try to say the right things, even though I often don't. I get impatient sometimes with students. They are so blessed—they're white!—so I don't want them to complain. Then I think of a black acquaintance who questioned me about teaching at a "white" university when "the black community needs you more."

He still believes that white institutions aren't themselves ever in need. That white students have it easy. That white students are transcendent. That their options are endless. That the world waits at their feet with doors that swing wide at their approach. That their schooling and "advantage" leave them whole and actualized and complete.

Believe that if you will. Or consider what I have seen.

I've seen students from small American towns and large American cities with worry on their faces.

Some of them know that according to cultural mythology, because they are white, they are supposed to be America's best and brightest. But, like me, they are imperfect after all.

They need rent money and refresher English and understanding parents and loving spouses and faculty who can remember their names. Some need self-confidence and courage. Some just need faith. The seniors need a break; many are suffering burnout. They've worked ungodly hours for cheapskate wages at extra jobs to pay their way. They are tired and the jig is not yet up. There are more papers to write, more semesters to go. More professors to please.

And there's no silver bullet.

So I nod soberly as a talented young man from a small Iowa town faces me across my desk and worries that he won't find a job after graduation because he is white and male.

"Nobody wants us anymore," he says. And part of me wants to say, yes that's right. But part of me can't because it isn't true and, besides, it's not the issue anyway. "People want talent," I tell him. "You're talented. But you have to define your talent by your 'difference'—in the language of 'diversity.' What's 'unique' about you? Articulate that in this market and you're as desirable as the next person."

He nods. "That's a good answer." It makes sense, even for him. He is the brother of a gay man dying of AIDS. He is a white boy who plays mean blues in a jazz band on weekend nights. He grew up poor and hungry but smart. And he writes like an angel. That's different enough for anybody. Conformity, indeed, is the bigger danger.

Of course, these lessons aren't on any syllabus—so that makes them suspect and makes an outsider like me a rebel and a barbarian, treading with soiled feet and dangerous ideas on hallowed and sacred ground—this precious academy. This fragile world. This fearful place.

The mail again. Arrogance and insult in two sentences:

"Reference your recent article in USA WEEKEND, could you please send a resume? I have a client, a graduate of Colorado, who believes you got access and a promotion based on a quota system."

And more mail:

"Your people use racism as an excuse for everything that happens you don't agree with. I suppose that had you not been hired for the position you now hold, it would also of [sic] been racism. You were probably hired as a quota."

It is fall.

A pretty Jewish girl from back East, a junior in my reporting class, wants to tell me something.

"I kissed a black man for the first time in my life last weekend—after a concert."

She reddens and giggles. She twists her pony tail.

She is perky and very smart. Quick, blond, alert. Her parents are both professionals—genuine good liberals who preached tolerance. Her open-mindedness makes her interesting but maybe reckless. She lingers after a class, wanting to tell me her latest escapade.

"You know how you hear this stuff about black people— how they're so superior sexually—almost like they're a different species or something?"

I nod, waiting.

This is hard for her to say. She giggles some more, twisting her hair. A couple of other students turn back to listen.

We are all watching her. "Well, I was at this concert with this guy—this black guy—and he started kissing me, and well, I was expecting this, you know, this great sexual moment!"

She giggles again.

We are watching her, still waiting.

She shrugs her shoulders. Her smile fades.

"It was like kissing a white guy."

She says it again, in case we missed her point.

"It was like kissing a *white guy!*"

She blinks and grins, ending her story with one final, sad note:

"I was so disappointed."

It is spring. I'm working on an essay explaining why I teach white students. At first I said it was because these students are young and they don't know enough. About life or themselves or other people.

But it turns out that nobody ever knows enough. The world is big and most of us perceive so little of its workings, its machinery—social and political, or otherwise.

Yet, my students are smart. They have traveled, many of them, to faraway places. They have done things I'll never try—water skiing and hang gliding and sailing and snowboarding and sunbathing on topless beaches. But the world is deep and the invisible people of subcultures are often hidden from their bright eyes.

And that blind spot worries me like a bad rash.

So I am naive enough, perhaps, to believe that my presence in the classroom, if nothing else, is a direct challenge to the stereotypical attitudes some of them still hold. But it turns out that they challenge my own stereotypical attitudes. So, in the end, all of us learn something from each other. My being here forces us each to cross a bridge and stretch.

That is why I teach white students.

To close the distance. I want to get close enough to the people I've feared and envied and hated, because nearness has a funny way of dispelling old demons.

We sit there, indeed, facing each other with different tapes playing in each of our heads. And amazingly, we often understand each other. It is not always pretty or perfect; cultural dissonance can be loud—and it is demanding. It asks me to teach Kristin and Heather and Kelly when I grew up with Carletha and Darlana and Leticia. It asks me not to slur my words. But my tongue trips over my past, and order eludes me. I can't stick to the clock or a syllabus. I need more minutes and more freedom, less structure and fewer rules. Still, most days it works. The teaching happens. And sometimes the teaching is good. The critics would be dismayed.

But so am I some days. I am trying my hand in a world that distrusts me from the outside in. So I am a dilettante. Playing dress-up in a field of dreams and, sometimes, falling flat on my face. And sometime soaring like the avatar. The journey is not steady. I travel it holding my breath.

Does it matter that I'm black?

It matters, but it matters more that I am mortal. I am not exemplary or celestial. I just teach, or try to. And on the days I fail, I have to look at my own flaws, not theirs.

I teach on all days, indeed, under this dark covering, and my students must penetrate that barrier in order to learn from me. They must, some of them, therefore, reorder their thinking about people who look like me. And I must do the same for them.

That is a racial milestone. Maybe even a miracle.

That is why I teach white students.

I want us to make a few miracles; then I'll watch them stride away and, in turn, make some new miracles of their own. Despite the cynics and the critics. And despite our fears.

* * *

That first spring on graduation day, as I met proud families on the lawn outside Macky Hall, the alarmists seemed a distant and outdated batch, in fact.

Instead, here were parents with cameras and corsages and smiles of pride. Here were spouses who paid the bills and fed the babies while husbands or wives, and daughters or sons, pursued their possible dreams.

They'd come from Kansas and Missouri and Illinois and Arkansas, from Colorado towns like Burlington and Denver and Sterling and Ouray. They seemed honest, good people with strong dreams and savings accounts that had lasted the race.

The day was theirs and it felt good.

Their loved ones had survived—even thrived, in some cases—even with dangerous trespassers like me and other dark faculty around.

They had tested the waters of change and nobody drowned.

And color, it turned out, hadn't mattered for *everything*. That's the plain truth, and sometimes ordinary people need to remind ourselves: Most people are more alike than they are different. There is always, thus, a reason for hope. Even in racial times. Especially in hateful seasons.

And so the current ugliness must pass. False alarms lose their cunning. Cooler heads prevail. Wisdom walks in, and sits down to stay awhile.

But will *I* stay? I may not. I've satisfied my purpose in coming here, to share a piece of myself with my white students—or, to prove that I could do it. I'm all done now, in fact, with proving things to white people because they are white. I'll need another reason now to stick around.

So maybe I will go. Or I'll settle in, maybe, just because I actually want to be here. Certainly the pressure is all gone, released by the clear, direct spirit of forgiveness. I've forgiven myself for rushing onto this campus for the wrong reasons. Forgiven others for asking me here, maybe for the wrong reasons, too.

I've moved the dirt here, found out why I'm here, and now it's time for a new stage. And the platform's rising.

Surely for us all, the next stop is higher ground.

CHAPTER TWELVE

The Affirmation

The dream is real my friends. The failure to make it
work is the unreality.
Toni Cade Bambera, The Salt Eaters, *1980*

"Let's be pretty tonight."

A friend is on the phone, and we are planning for a party.
We are going with our husbands to a fancy-dress dance, and we
are dreaming about the evening.

"Let's be pretty tonight," she says, and her proposal releases
a torrent of womanish chatter—talk of glittery earrings and
sheer stockings, bare skin and lace, and perfume.

She will wear black velvet toreador pants with a black lace-
mesh halter, a matador jacket and high-heel shoes. I will wear
high heels, too, and a long black velvet sheath with white lace
sleeves and a beaded bodice cut low and off the shoulders.

My dress is two years old. But I've never worn it since I

bought it, so it feels new. I feel new when I put it on, after a cool shower and long rubdown with a clean fresh towel. Then I pull the dress over my head and the silk lining slides over my skin like spring water.

This is a lovely gown and my breasts swell out of it—a brown woman's abundance; in the past, something to hide, to camouflage, to bind down tight. But when I walk down the stairs to the living room, my husband grabs me by the waist and kisses me on the lips, on my face, in my hair. You'll mess up everything, I tell him.

No I won't, he says. We are laughing.

At the hotel, inside the ballroom, I find my friend and she, too, is laughing tonight and so is her husband. He likes his wife in the toreador pants and the lace mesh and the high heels, and he is teasing her, too, and pulling her toward him, embracing her and smelling her hair, her perfume.

We like this festiveness, and we are feeling something good, all of us—but my friend and I especially. We are feeling what it's like to love ourselves—two brown women, born to an era that said we were all wrong.

Tonight we are right.

Everything about us is—not just our party clothes and our hair and our bright lipstick, not just all of that, but our understanding is right. We can be pretty tonight, and we can know it. It takes a long time for a brown woman to know that, or maybe even other women—other *people*—as well. It takes hard work and self-permission and self-love.

I am liking it a lot—this new feeling, of not making excuses or worrying that something bad is reeking from my presence.

I am a good person, a loving wife, a strong mother, a good friend, a kind daughter, a loyal sister. And some days, life should be a fantasy. I can decide that right now, even for tonight.

So for tonight:

I am put together with stardust and good blood and fine genes, with the continuous urgings and tender pushes from ancestors and old friends and even the newly departed—loved ones, every one.

I have a strong body, carved out of ebony and Jurassic amber, bronze and hard iron. My eyes are cut from diamonds. My hair is woven from the cattails of the Blue Nile, the hair under my arms and on my legs and between my legs are leaves of the konker tree and my eyelashes are the feathers of the great heron and my blood is the juice of pomegranates and my muscles are the haunches of the leopard and my joints are the knees of mountain goats and the elbows of elephants and my feet are onyx, planted solid on a rock, or sometimes eagle's wings, lifting me up, up, up to soar and dip and fly.

I smell like the Earth and like the sweat of a fertile bride waiting for her virile groom and like all the flowers that ever bloomed and ever will bloom again and again. My heart is generous, so filled with forgiveness and hope that I can sing to children and shelter old women and hold old men in my arms and wipe away the regrets in their tears.

I can swim the Mediterranean Sea and scale McKinley and Badille and Kilimanjaro and Aconcagua, and I can ride St. Mary's glacier from her icy heights, across blue valleys as wide as rivers, and dip gracefully into the mouths of green lakes and call the trout and the rock bass and the walleye, and hear their words when they answer.

I am blessed by Jesus and I know the stories of Buddha and Brahma, the creator god, and Vishnu, the sleeping god, whose dream is the universe, and Horus and Isis and Osiris, and Gilgamesh, and Shiri ya Mwari, the Bird of God, and Shirichena, the Bird of Bright Plumage, and Mithra, the god of light, and Orpheus, called "the Fisher" who fishes men, and Mumbo, the serpent god, and Shiva, who dances the holy dance. And I behold the Cross, and ponder the Holy Grail and the Net of Indra, and I sit in the center of the Wheel of Fortune, anchored so firmly. And, like the Navajo, otherwise called the Dineh, I am on the pollen path. That heavenly pollen path.

Beauty above me, beauty below me, beauty to the left of me, beauty to the right of me, beauty before me. I am, like the Navajo, on the pollen path.

And I am pretty tonight.

No one in this room tonight is an enemy. They are all allies because I command it. They are all comrades because I believe it. They are all compatriots because we are all fighting for justice, goodness, and truth, and I mandate our mutual respect and understanding. If their deeds cause harm to anyone, I approach the offenders with love. If they won't hear my protest, I will melt their hearts with persistent love, with undying faith in their potential to be righteous and holy.

I know these things because I have the knowledge of the ages at my right hand and the wisdom of the universe at my left hand. And peace flows in me like a deep, blue river that I mount like a stallion and ride and ride into everlasting.

Now some will laugh at these things. They doubt such capacity, question such serenity, distrust such authority. But tonight when I take to the dance floor, can I help it if the parquet under my feet turns to gold and my onyx feet in a flash are transformed to eagle's wings and I then fly around the dance space, spinning and soaring and turning, moving to music composed just for me? It was written before I was born and I recognize it instantly, even before the first note is struck. It's my music, but I am filled with generosity, so I want to share it, to dance it with the others who've been waiting to move, longing to shake and jump and turn and roll.

So I pull a woman with yellow hair from her seat and she grabs her husband, a man with black eyes, and he grabs a man with a kinky red beard and that man grabs his friend, an old woman with flowered skirts and seven teeth and a smile wide with knowledge and wisdom, who grabs a child who grabs her mother who grabs *her* mother who grabs an uncle who grabs his wife of forty years who reaches out both her hands to a line of people too long to count. All of them step onto the dance floor with me, all of them dipping and turning and rolling, and we are a great happy party—dancing and feeling our bodies and letting the sweat pour off our bodies. Our glistening sweat, shining like diamonds in the night.

We are dancing, yes we are.

Dancing like the Ladakhi and the Apache and the Dineh.

Dancing for all the years we didn't dance, certainly not together. Dancing to reclaim all the lost chances, all the harsh words, all the bad juju that ever passed between us. Dancing the future and its hopes into being.

I wave to my friend and she lifts her hands, acknowledging the truth of what I am seeing—nodding her head, yes!, you are right. These things are true.

I hear her laughter across the room, and I catch it in my mouth and swallow it and the warmth of it is like a ballast that sets me right, lifting me even higher, making me twirl and whoop and sparkle in this beautiful, beautiful night.

From the heights, I watch myself dance, marveling at my grace and at my strong arms and lovely neck and my clear eyes and my remarkable strength.

I am stronger than a Sepik crocodile, more cunning than

Gideon's three hundred, more powerful than David's five stones, brighter than the thunderbolts of Zeus.

I can change lives, resolve injustice, reverse poverty, inspire hearts and minds, connect kindred souls. I can make laughter and inspire singing, persuade lovers to find each other, strangers to make friends, and enemies to make peace. I can move mountains.

And God has given me permission to say these things, and to write these things.

I will thus now, emboldened with the spirit of the ages, preach the good news to the poor, heal the brokenhearted, teach deliverance to the captives, recover sight to the blind, and set at liberty those that are bruised and defeated.

I can even tame a lion, snare it and pin it on its back and hold it down, until its bravado is quieted, its heavy breathing not even a whisper, its roar only soft breathing—more quiet than a hummingbird waiting to fly, softer than dew.

Every morning I wash the sky and sing the clouds aloft.

Then I drink in the sunshine and I glow.

So it makes perfect sense, perfect logic.

I am pretty tonight. And these are the words, borrowed from Joseph Campbell, a white man, the myth man—who borrowed it, in turn, from his heroes and dreamers, his seers and shamans, then passed it on to believers such as me to describe this special night.

"Oh . . . ah . . ."

CHAPTER THIRTEEN

Setting to Right

Please forgive us. Please release and please set into the depths of the ocean our *pilikia* (trouble), nevermore to rise. All this we ask in Thy holy name. Amen.
E. Victoria Shook, Ho'oponopono: Contemporary Uses of a Hawaiian Problem-Solving Process

Finally, now, I would go to Mississippi—to meet with the ghosts and work out any final puzzles, walk the soil that birthed my father, drop some holy water on the red clay and make full peace. This was my picture of a proper ending. My journey, and this journal, would close where it began, in the hot clay roots of my history. And this trek would be a right thing, and good. I sent for a map and circled the hot spots. I would now be ready. I couldn't wait.

But I didn't go yet to Mississippi, or even get close—not this trip, anyway. Instead I rushed to the other side of the world, and almost fell off.

I flew on a bird to Hawaii.

God sends us where He wants. Best we just get ready, get up and go.

The plane set down in Honolulu at 4:00 P.M. on a placid August afternoon. The breezes, those trade winds, blow off the ocean almost all the time on these islands—this one called Oahu, an old name but new to my mouth. So I landed, and right away something felt different.

There's a smell in warm places that captures all the odors of living and growing things. This smell was sweet but light. It was there or *here,* then gone for a time. But it always hurried back. I might've tasted it on my tongue. It was flowers, or maybe just the air. I breathed it in. I watched the setting sun. Something would happen here.

A conference at the University of Hawaii had brought me to Honolulu and the timing had felt all wrong. I was "busy," with my explorations—trying to discover my father's rightful legacies and my history and find my place, and write about it all—and now near the end of my odyssey I had to stop and travel 3,500 miles, most of it across the vast, implacable Pacific, and make like a scholar. And also, to my surprise, I detected old fears— worries about hotel clerks with surprised looks and restaurants with bad tables in noisy, tight corners. And Hawaii seemed like an unlikely place. I'd have to defend myself for even being here.

I will just watch, I decided. I will just listen.

So I opened my eyes in paradise. And God allowed me to see and hear and know many things:

First, I saw brown people—at every turn, tens of thousands of them. Colored people. Dark people, with all those names we still know: light-skin, red-bone, caramel, cinnamon, high yellow, near white, blue black, Chinese-looking (but, here, they were indeed Chinese), Indian-looking (and they were, indeed, Indian), honey-color, lemon-color, ebony black, coal black, skillet blond, tar baby, *black* black.

They all seemed busy and not worried, at ease and fully and comfortably dark. They were being themselves. Wearing *their* clothes—hair *not* straightened, bodies *not* girdled or covered or shrouded, skin *not* shielded from the tropical sun, lips *not* pinched. Noses wide. Being themselves. And the mix—Filipino American, Japanese American, Chinese American, Hawaiian American, African American, Samoan, Fijian, Tahitian, Tongoan; I couldn't even identify all the many, many folks—was like being held close. Sweet, this feeling—like finding an old loved one around every corner, in every shop, at every stoplight. I'm exaggerating. No, I'm trying to get this right. Almost everybody, to one degree or another, looked like they could belong to me. Or that I could belong to them—be their loved one. Or even be their friend. But if I doubted, I could confirm our sweet affiliation—just by stepping up.

I suppose I should've made some higher discovery right off. But *first,* importantly, there was the shock and joy of not being alien. Suddenly indeed, right there, very quickly, on that first afternoon in that place, it felt so natural to be colored. Nobody turned and stared, or looked surprised or alarmed. And I melted into this scene, just washed into it—of course, like the waves foaming up onto the shoreline and disappearing into the beige silk sand.

Listen.

For a person on the margin, such a moment can transform. It is a turning point, existentially, and *must* be saluted. Comedian Richard Pryor did it best perhaps in a stand-up routine, delivered bravely after his first trip to Africa:

"... And I was sitting in a hotel, and a voice said to me, he said, 'Look around. What do you see?' and I said, 'I see all colors of people doing everything, you know.' And the voice said, 'Do you see any niggers?' ... And I said, 'No.' And I said, 'You know why? 'Cause there aren't any.' And it hit me like a shot. Man, I started crying and shit. I was sitting there, I said, 'Yeah, I've been here three weeks. I haven't even said it. I haven't even thought it.' And it made me say, 'Oh, my God, I've been wrong. I've been wrong. I got to regroup ... I mean, I said, I ain't gonna *never* call another black man "nigger." ' "

The audience wasn't laughing at this point. Some people might've even cried as Pryor spun out his beautiful epiphany.

Do you see any niggers?

On that island, out there in the middle of the vastly unperturbed Pacific, surrounded by hued people, all of them unapologetically dark—in a state with the least number of *white* people of the fifty United States—I didn't see any niggers.

It's a state of mind.

It's also a matter of sight. In Denver, when I was growing up, I was nearly full grown before I realized I didn't have to go to the Rocky Mountains to *see* the Rocky Mountains. Some blessed people in Denver, and in areas nearby, lived in houses on top of hills and on top of mesas, with vistas. On Gaylord Street, where I lived, I could see to the end of the block.

Dreams can't flourish in full understanding with such limitations. Imagination isn't that powerful. I was embarrassed, truly, to learn late in my childhood that the mountains were so close. I should have known.

Here in Hawaii, on one little island, I already knew three-quarters of the world's people are colored, but now I could see it. The sight of that ratio made me giddy. Here was a shred of

proof that I am not the outsider. In Hawaii, therefore, I rhapso-
dized over the color matter. My husband, who was with me on
this trip, indulged me—listening to me marvel about the racial
mosaic, hearing me celebrate the "beauty" of it.

And he waited.

And in a day or two, after I calmed down and recognized
some realities—that even in this so-called melting pot, there are
problems—he and others helped me see the whole picture.

That first Sunday morning, he bought me a local newspaper.
An article quoted the complaints of local teens who couldn't
wait to grow up and leave the islands for "the mainland." Not
enough energy here, one said. Not enough competition. Too isolated. Too provincial. Later that evening, I met a father—a
transplant from Michigan—who understood their worry. He
said Hawaii had been a good choice for him. But for his children, who were born and grew up here, the islands had been too
remote and, also, too easy. So they're real good surfers, he said of
his teen boys, laughing, but implied that was the extent of their
interests. What more, indeed, should a child need to know in a
paradise without seasons?

Plenty, it turns out.

There is racial strife. Native Hawaiians, it turns out, are not
only the poorest people here—they are the fewest in number,
least educated, least employed, least healthy of all groups on the
islands. And many are angry—not willing to forget that sugar
barons and their backers "stole" their country in 1893, over-
throwing the last ruling Hawaiian monarch, Queen Liliuokalani, in a clearly illegal takeover reportedly carried out by 162
U.S. Marines.

The Marines put her under house arrest in the Iolani Palace
in Honolulu, where the devoutly Christian queen wrote hymn
lyrics and quiet, lilting poetry.

So now, one century later, a nationalist movement has sprung up—seeking to reclaim the islands from American sovereignty, or at least to return self-rule and land to native Hawaiians. Widespread empathy for the cause has grown, even from perhaps unlikely places. A recent president of the Hawaii Hotel Association, for example, noted, "This is a community-wide issue." This man, Murray Towill, quoted in the *Los Angeles Times* in January 1993, added, "There was a wrong committed with the overthrow that needs to be corrected. The whole community, including the visitor industry ... needs to be supportive, make sure that we are all aware of it, understand the issues."

As a visitor, I had no choice but to understand.

Activists at tourist stops were selling T-shirts promoting the "Kingdom of Hawaii." And before the week was out during my visit, local authorities arrested a key nationalist activist, alleging he harbored a tax fugitive. Local newspapers put the story on page one. Meanwhile, one Honolulu radio station, awash in native music, promoted itself as "Radio Free Hawaii." The sound of impatient people was making itself heard.

Trouble in paradise. I shouldn't have been surprised. Trouble, indeed—or *pilikia,* as the Hawaiians say it—is the way of the world. I see that now. I was looking, all this time, for a life without trouble, where racial strife especially would get resolved, once and for all. But, on this side of heaven, there is no such place. Conflict is inevitable. But of course, and why not? We are barbarians. No evil, it seems, is beneath the human heart. And our human history with all its many martyrs and its holocausts and its horrors is our calling card. But if we are honest, and God knows I've tried to be here, we are convinced—even if secretly—that making peace is the better way.

So in Honolulu, which for now would be my Mississippi, I

wasn't really surprised to find yet another method for mending broken relationships. (All over the world, the work goes on.) In Hawaii, the process has a bouncy, lyrical name that at first I couldn't pronounce. It's *ho'oponopono*. It's spoken with a hiccup and hard *o*'s.

I frowned when I first heard the word from the great cross-cultural trainer, Dr. Paul Pedersen, a facilitator at the conference I was attending. So his suggestion that I investigate this technique carried weight. I took notes, but asked stupid questions. Can you spell it? How do you say it again? I'm sure I sounded clueless and besotted, slightly infatuated with this "native" knowledge. But I was intrigued, or maybe I felt affirmed to discover that everywhere, it seems, folks are trying to mend fences.

Ho'oponopono—meaning "setting to right"—is a meeting ritual, designed to maintain harmony and solve conflict within a family. I let the odd word settle on my lips and in the back of my head, a topic to study later. But it kept coming up. The next time was that weekend from a tour guide—talking into a scratchy microphone on a tour van—describing for his load of passengers the Hawaiian Nine Virtues. ". . . And No. 9 is *ho'oponopono*."

My ears perked up.

"It's the Hawaiian way . . . settling inner-family conflict," he said, his microphone crackling nearly every syllable. I strained to hear better. "It's the understanding . . . problems will come up, but . . . can be settled . . . You know, it's . . . keep the family going. Keep everybody . . . and together."

At the next stop, I cornered him with questions.

What's this *ho'oponopono*?

The man brightened, taking me by the elbow. He was Filipino and Chinese, he said, and worked during the week at a small local company. Driving a tour van was his weekend job, to help pay his daughter's expenses at the prestigious King Kamehameha School in Honolulu. She was an honor student, he added proudly, and had been accepted at a school on the mainland, the University of Oregon in Portland. "Get your education! That's what I always tell her."

I listened, waiting impatiently for him to move the talking back to my subject—this *ho'oponopono.*

"It's the Hawaiian way," he finally said. ". . . solving your family trouble. Your disagreements—big ones, little ones," he said. "You never go to bed angry at each other. Always work things out."

In your family, do you do this?

Always, the man said. "You never go to bed angry. Always keep the family working. Always solve your troubles."

Things don't have to be as they are.

In Molokai or in Mississippi, bad blood can get fixed, if the heart is right. People everywhere know that. But the heart, so often, is wrong. So in Hawaii, the *ho'oponopono* starts with a prayer, of course, or a *pule,* asking God or the "powers that be" for help in solving the family trouble. Then, according to a book on the subject, family members sit together in a circle or around a table, and they state the problem. Then they discuss it. They talk about all the miscues and goofs. Unraveling everything. And they confess any wrongs, even offering to restitute, if needed.

Then they forgive one another, releasing one another from "the negative entanglements" that held them.

My bus driver said the "release" is powerful. Of course.

I've tried to harness some of that power, releasing all my old demons, letting them fly. At least I perceive that I better understand the power of this positive behavior—even if it always will be hard to carry off. Maybe that's why in these Hawaii family meetings, in the final moments, there's a *pani*—where the problem is declared closed, "never to be brought up again," said my sourcebook. Finally there's a closing prayer, to reestablish harmony with God or the supernatural powers, and to ask forgiveness from God, too.

Please forgive us. Please release and please set into the depths of the ocean our pilikia, *nevermore to rise. All this we ask in Thy holy name. Amen.*

This was all beautiful, so I wanted to claim the ritual for me, but it couldn't be fully mine. My family wouldn't try it—they told me. It's somebody else's practice, they said. And anyway this ritual was only for blood matters, for families, not for nations or communities or for the world. In the end, I could only be glad about it—affirmed to discover that all over the little blue earth, folks are on a quest like mine. Trying to bind up. They don't ever stop trying. And it never ends—the trouble. But you keep working on it. And over time, the "poker-hot rage" of dissension, as one black writer once described racial discord, finally abates.

So now I am home again, back from a very long journey. And I am now afraid.

Without my anger turned to high, will I be flush and urgent and strong? Without my belly swollen with bile, will I be *relevant?*

Such a dilemma, indeed. But my question makes me smile, and that's a good sign. Maybe I'm finally close to the truth—that forgiveness is surely fully impossible. You just work on it, and the working is what's good.

I must work, indeed, on my race hate with the careful attention of an archaeologist scraping away the dust from old bones. It's painstaking some days, other times a breeze. But I keep at it, knowing that what's underneath the ancient grime might be dented and broken, but certainly it needs to get cleaned.

I need to try.

It isn't easy, because forgiving the racial past means, first, acknowledging that it happened, and that means reviving old horrors. Nobody wants to do that. No one wishes to be "plunged, head down," as James Baldwin put it, "into the torrent of what [one] does not remember and does not wish to remember." But you can't forgive something you haven't struggled with, toiled over, walked on, slept with—and race is a bad bed partner. There's no comfortable way to lie down with it.

That's why I must forget my racial past. Give it up, even though that asks so much of me, all my aces.

But I must try, knowing that like a bad penny the bad feelings and mean ways will rise and rise again. But now I can pray. I can hope and I will believe that I can overcome. There's just nothing else.

In this manner, we remake ourselves, every twenty-four hours, praying as Jesus and the saints and Buddha and all the other holy warriors taught us: "Give us *this* day . . ."

That is the pace, one day at a time. Forgiveness must renew itself because this is a long war, and we're all in it. Forgiveness, indeed, is not a feeling—it is a decision.

Nelson Mandela knew that when he left the Victor Verster prison, after twenty-seven years in South African jails, locked up for his convictions and his color. "I greet you all in the name of *peace* . . . ," he began, knowing no other word would suffice for the crowds waiting to hear him. Mandela wasn't the first to have this understanding. Deep in the Pacific, the last queen of Hawaii followed her captors to her quarters. Then this Liliuokalani wrote a song for her followers, again with a necessary statement:

"Forgive with loving kindness . . . that we may be made

pure." It is a simple request, but it doesn't tamp down all the important questions: Must I forgive? Should, indeed, I forget? And can I love? And should I try?

I can't fully dissect the layers of such exquisite questions. But I finally have an answer:

Yes.

It's more than a proper ending.

This is how I begin.

EPILOGUE

Good Medicine

When they say come and sing, that's the medicine.
Ella Fitzgerald, in Jet *magazine, June 27, 1988*

Just one more look. Remember it, Daddy? That summer you drove us to Salt Lake City? Really we were on our way to California, *Disneyland*. Lauretta and I were stupid with excitement. Two sisters, one at fifteen a gawky teenager—and me still ten and between everything. Not a little kid. Not old enough to be more, and kind of frustrated by that. And Mama reading from the map.

There was some green medicine I had to take every morning that tasted awful, like dead leaves or old aluminum. Or maybe it tasted worse—vile stuff in a bottle with a white prescription label taped on the front. One teaspoon every day after breakfast, until the bottle was empty. It took weeks of daily doses to finish off. I can't even remember what illness I had, requiring this green syrup to ruin my summer vacation. But Mama, always so intensely concerned about her girls, was relentless with it.

Here's your medicine, holding out the spoon.

Every morning in a different motel, I'd wake up excited about the day's travels. Then I'd remember the green medicine—indeed, I remember this trip mostly in association with that medicine. It stood like a tall mountain between every new day and the fun it promised. It seemed like a cheap trick, something cruel to ruin a kid's summer break.

Happiness never comes without strings.

We learn that young.

But you were trying, Daddy. What else would make a young father pack up the car and drive west to see an ocean and a TV mouse? And you weren't a frivolous man.

The year was 1959.

The desert West was still big and empty. The people there were slightly cockeyed with the newness of it. They'd arrived so fast and thrown up their little trailers and cafés and curio shops. Everyone looked surprised to be there. Most people wanted either to be rich or to be left alone.

Nobody asked too many questions. And it hardly ever rained. If this Western desert wasn't perfect for a black man—and it wasn't—it was the best a young father could do.

Disneyland had been open just four years. It was still a new attraction. To see it fresh, before rich people had used it up and gotten tired of it, made it a charmed destination. A thousand miles at least stood between us and the Magic Kingdom, but every mile promised something beautiful to look on.

And soon, before we were ready to believe our eyes, there

were the Mormon Tabernacle and the nearby Mormon Temple, a granite monument groaning toward the sky.

Only a dreamer takes his daughter to see such sights, knowing she's not then sought after by that assemblage, not in 1959, even if she wanted to join up—which I didn't—but taking her up to the front door anyway. Letting her peek in.

There was uncommon air in Salt Lake City—an odd softness to everything. The climate is dry like Denver's, but the touch of moisture—rising off the big lake—cuts the edge off the dryness. I don't think I even broke a sweat there. During our short stay, we wore nice smiles and dry clothes. And, strangely, there was a feeling there of safety.

I've since, on reflection, decided it wasn't at all safety that I was feeling. Instead I know now, Daddy, that you were simply relaxed. This trip wouldn't insult you. This wasn't the deep South. We could take pictures and go fishing and sightsee without questions. Your ease, as we traveled, lent an overlay of calm to the days. Mama now recalls that trip with one urgent word: *pleasant.*

We stayed in a kitchenette motel.

Orange cotton curtains covered the windows. The rooms glowed every hour, almost like daybreak round the clock. For the two short days we stayed there, I awakened in the orange-colored mist, dressed and ate corn flakes and milk, then choked down the vile green medicine. The day now could start.

I had my own camera, a cheap little Kodak, and during the two weeks of that vacation I peered through the tiny lens and snapped the Grand Canyon and the Golden Gate Bridge and Grauman's Chinese Theatre and the California Redwood Forest. We saw a tree there that was big enough to drive our '54

Dodge right through its trunk. At the curio shop, we bought postcards.

But first there was Salt Lake City, where we were oddities, but amazingly nobody seemed to worry about us much. Maybe everybody in Utah back then was kind of off kilter, far removed from their origins. Or preoccupied with their religion. And we were just passing through—most white people seemed to like that—gazing at the pretty parks, the city pools, the suntanned people.

The second or third day, we went out to the lake.

From a distance, it was blue and endless. The sight, to a girl reared on the dry high plains, close to rocky mountains, made my heart rush. In a word, the water was a *possibility*.

That's what you gave us, Daddy. You planted that seed every time you piled us in the Dodge and headed for a rock with a name on it or a pond with a pretty shore. God only knows where that came from, your faith that, ultimately, was a kind of belief in America—despite everything.

Those places you took us to see were so big, like America herself. A child trapped in a closed place must have trouble envisioning such beauty and dreams. So I marvel, Daddy, that in spite of many good reasons to feel cheated and trapped, you kept trying and driving and looking forward. Something better was always just *there!* over the horizon.

We started out right after breakfast. In keeping with your style, we were cleaned and groomed and the green stuff had been choked down—whatever it took to keep a daughter healthy and alive—and the day now was properly ready to begin.

We had a picnic packed and wore swimming suits under our clothes. And there before us was the big blue water, shimmying like a mirage.

"Well look at that," you said, in your quiet way, but excited I think to show us something else new and big. We drove forever it seemed, gazing at the water, then smelling the saltiness, and then the water was closer and then it was real. Right before us.

Seabirds filled the sky, squawking at each other. Lauretta and I, sitting on the back seat of the Dodge, each threw open a car door and started for the water. I held my camera, ready to snap. I wanted forever perhaps to capture the pitch of your straight back, just there in front of me.

You'd made a promise: We would float in the Great Salt Lake, bob on the surface like corks. Salt in the lake was so dense, you said, we simply couldn't drown.

I was always a stone in water, awkward in odd ways, sinking and splashing. I couldn't swim. So this was a large promise. You vowed today that I would float.

So you took me to the water. A daddy does this.

Then the surprise.

The awful smell. It was more than salty. The water was briny and sulfurous—a stench with its own queer, sour presence. Black flies, appearing suddenly, swarmed at our ankles, near our faces.

Mama called us up short. Wait a minute. Come back here. Don't go. She has always been cautious about her girls, in contrast to your quiet and demanding fearlessness. So we held back, but looking to you, we waited for a signal. You'd stopped in your tracks, just gazing now at the water, rolling a toothpick in your teeth. You looked disappointed, but also disgusted—but also not surprised.

Funny how the unexpected can feel personal. A closed door. Bad weather when it spoils things. The odd reminder, even when certain people feel happy and safe, can make them newly aware that they aren't members of the chosen people. And now here was dour proof, a smelly obstacle.

This was a problem. A promise would get broken.

Slowly you turned for the car, tossing down your toothpick. We were leaving. Mama, holding the picnic things in her lap, shifted on her seat, not answering our questions. She didn't know how the day would be salvaged. You would decide. She always let you decide.

Call it trust.

She loved you.

If a woman ever loved a man, she loved you loyally—standing firmly at your wing. You ruled the roost. But her uncanny touch blessed everything. So, together, you and she were twin rocks, planted on either side. Looking out for danger.

I'm reminded how the winter before, when a "bad" girl chased me home from school one day, pelting me upside the head finally with one solid snowball fortified with a rock, Mama walked me to the girl's house—to settle the score. That's what I thought. But when the tough girl came out to her porch, Mama looked her over, then gently pulled the child into her arms and simply asked a question: "What's wrong, baby? Why did you do this?"

This hard girl, tough as nails, heard Mama's steady, soft voice, that Southern softness—felt the warm arms holding her close, granting her love and simple forgiveness—and the girl instantly started crying, tears running like rushing water. She was melting into the acceptance of a human touch, not caring that I—who'd fled her threats only an hour before—was watching, gape-eyed, while she blubbered now like a baby. Then Mama, pointing to me, firmly told the girl that "Patricia isn't your enemy"—in fact, I would be her friend. *I would?* Mama looked at me solidly and her eyes firmly answered. She knew, Daddy, that's what you'd want her to say.

And now it was summer and she was waiting for your signal. I can see her in her shorts and swimming suit, sleek and brown—a better swimmer than you, truthfully, but letting you control the moment. She must have known. Or she believed. Or she understood.

You weren't in control of this. Nothing you could do would turn the foul, briny water into a fresh lake. And it wasn't your fault. But disappointments for colored people often felt as if we'd caused them, or at least deserved them. Bad moments like this could make us feel stupid. *Didn't you know this water was wretched?* Maybe that's what we were asking each other, even asking you—with our eyes, with our complaints.

I was whining. *Let's go find a swimming pool. Please let's go do something fun.*

But you were in charge that day, as always, and we spent the afternoon instead at a park and knew we'd better be happy about it. Once, years later, I spent a summer wanting to believe that you happily, and magically, took us to a sparkling pool that day and taught me how to float, as you'd promised. But you didn't. That would've been a Hollywood movie ending, and such a lovely memory.

But life isn't a fantasy.

It's hard work. Then it gives us choices. So I choose now not to judge us for whatever missteps we made on days like that day. Surely, we were pioneers, rambling around out there in the briny West. And we looked odd, in the eyes of others. And I'll seem odd now, looking for blessed ways to heal it all and get over what has haunted me.

A strong potion will heal, however. Steady doses mend up

old wounds. Daddy, you understood that clearly. As well, you were a realist and you knew what I now finally see:

Some days there aren't happy endings.

But always there are *new* days. The next morning, you claimed yours.

You packed us in the Dodge and we kept on heading West.

And when you started up the car, Daddy, you were whistling. Just softly. Just enough.

I can hear it now. A high, thin melody forced between your teeth. It wafted over our heads as we drove down the road, away from the Great Salt Lake, away from an afternoon's disappointment, headed toward our high dreams, trusting we were going the right way.

ACKNOWLEDGMENTS

Now I thank my God and my Savior, and the sweet care of the Holy Spirit, for blessing me on this journey with these many kind helpers and friends:

Carla Mayer Glasser, my agent, whose steadfast and ongoing work on my behalf has never wavered.

Mindy Werner, my editor at Viking, whose discerning eye assisted me as much as her friendship and laughter. Some days, Mindy, the laughter indeed was what I needed most to keep on going.

My loving family who believed: my beautiful daughters, Joi and Alana, who patiently helped me work by sharing their ideas, encouragement, and wisdom; my loving and lovely sister, Dr. Lauretta Lyle, whose editing assistance was peerless and invaluable; my warm and honest cousin Dewitt White, who helped me search for truth; and my parents—my powerful mother, Nannie Ruth Burnett Smith, whose loving-kindness has sustained me all the days of my life, and my late, beloved father, William Amos Smith, whose expectations for me set a high mark that I will always honor. You are mighty people. Thank you, dear family, for blessing my life.

My many praying friends, especially Denise Materre, a sister sent from God, and Marsha Johnson, whose faith together helped keep me focused and looking up. Sister girls, look what God did!

And especially my loving husband, J. Daniel Raybon, who kept the lights burning and the prayers rising—and never once tired of reading every word with care and attention. Then, deep in winter, you closed the stubborn window. Sugar, that made all the difference. Have I told you that I love you?